NARRATIVE INQUIRY IN EARLY CHILDHOOD AND ELEMENTARY SCHOOL

Learning to Teach, Teaching Well

Stephanie Sisk-Hilton and Daniel R. Meier

Routledge
Taylor & Francis Group

NEW YORK AND LONDON

KH

First published 2017
by Routledge
711 Third Avenue, New York, NY 10017

and by Routledge
2 Park Square, Milton Park, Abingdon, Oxon OX14 4RN

Routledge is an imprint of the Taylor & Francis Group, an informa business

© 2017 Taylor & Francis

The right of Stephanie Sisk-Hilton and Daniel R. Meier to be identified as the authors of this work has been asserted by them in accordance with sections 77 and 78 of the Copyright, Designs and Patents Act 1988.

Library of Congress Cataloging in Publication Data
Names: Sisk-Hilton, Stephanie. | Meier, Daniel R.
Title: Narrative inquiry in early childhood and elementary school : learning to teach, teaching well / Stephanie Sisk-Hilton and Daniel R. Meier.
Description: New York : Routledge, 2017. | Includes bibliographical references and index.
Identifiers: LCCN 2016014254| ISBN 9781138924406 (hbk.) | ISBN 9781138924413 (pbk.) | ISBN 9781315684390 (e-book)
Subjects: LCSH: Narrative inquiry (Research method) | Education, Elementary. | Early childhood education.
Classification: LCC H61.295 .S57 2017 | DDC 372.072/3—dc23
LC record available at http://lccn.loc.gov/2016014254

ISBN: 978-1-138-92440-6 (hbk)
ISBN: 978-1-138-92441-3 (pbk)
ISBN: 978-1-315-68439-0 (ebk)

Typeset in Bembo
by diacriTech, Chennai

MIX
Paper from
responsible sources
FSC
www.fsc.org   FSC® C013056

Printed and bound in Great Britain by
TJ International Ltd, Padstow, Cornwall

10/18/17

For Michael and Patricia Sisk,
who taught me to value and love the stories around and within us
—Stephanie Sisk-Hilton

In memory of my parents
—Daniel R. Meier

CONTENTS

FOREWORD

On the Power and Possibilities of Making Sense of Children's Stories through Narrative Inquiry: An Invitation

Mariana Souto-Manning

Let me tell you a story. . . . Long, long ago, early childhood classrooms and elementary schools were filled with stories. Stories were created, told, rehearsed, and enacted by young children. They were proclaimed, read, and written by adults. Some of these stories became well-known standards in early childhood education. For example, the stories authored by Vivian Paley's student, "the boy who would be a helicopter" (1990). In such classrooms, children authored stories though play and authentic interactions, in purposeful ways (Souto-Manning & Martell, 2016). Storytelling was the heart of many classrooms and (pre)schools; after all, young children make sense of their lives through storytelling and regard it as "a site for problem solving" (Ochs, Smith, & Taylor, 1996, p. 95).

Then, academic demands were pushed down into the early grades and teachers started being evaluated not by their students or communities, not according to the complexity of the tasks negotiated by their students, but by so-called "objective" measures captured by numbers. Children's stories were marginalized and excluded from what counted as data—even if supported by other kinds of documentation. And although positioned in marginal ways to teaching and learning—at least according to official curricula and assessments in place—these stories are still alive! In early childhood and elementary classrooms, each "day, many problem solving narratives happen and delineate roles, relationships, values, and world-views" (Ochs et al., 1996, p. 95) for children and adults alike.

Daniel Meier and Stephanie Sisk-Hilton (henceforth Daniel and Stephanie) invite us to pay attention to the narratives authored by children's actions and interactions, to unveil their potential and position narratives as foundational to teaching and learning. They invite us to teach against the grain, to approach puzzling issues from the perspective of teacher-researchers who are agents of change. They encourage us to recognize how stories capture complexities in human interactions and get to the heart of humanity in ways that no number can. In doing so, they urge us to engage in "narrative inquiry *for* teaching" instead of "narrative inquiry *about* teaching" (Sisk-Hilton & Meier, 2016, p. 8).

In this book, stories matter. The stories shared capture and communicate varied and rich linguistic and cultural practices. *Narrative Inquiry in Early Childhood and Elementary School: Learning to Teach, Teaching Well* makes visible how stories need to be heard because they offer fertile grounds for teaching and learning. But while storytelling is certainly part of narrative inquiry, Daniel and Stephanie elucidate how narrative inquiry goes well beyond storytelling. They explain how narrative inquiry can inform teaching—when used to gather and analyze information and find (new) meanings in our teaching and in children's learning. They remind us how narrative inquiry can make teaching more culturally relevant (Ladson-Billings, 1995) and inclusive.

Classrooms are full of stories. And stories provide windows into children's learning and development. Poet Maya Angelou stated: "There is no greater agony than bearing an untold story inside you." Daniel and Stephanie propose that classroom narratives need not go untold in favor of standardized ways to measure learning. They affirm the need for stories to be told. After all, as Angelou proposed, there is no greater agony than knowing that a child's potential remains untold while being silenced by numbers that document deficits rather than assets. Telling the stories negotiated inside classrooms is a powerful and transformative act. As teachers, it is our moral responsibility to tell the stories of our classroom; the stories told, enacted, and actively coauthored by the children we teach. It is upon us to narrate more hopeful tomorrows.

But—how does one engage in narrative inquiry? Through rich examples from a variety of settings, Daniel and Stephanie address key questions, inviting readers to consider the power and possibility of narrative inquiry. They ask: what distinguishes a story (or storytelling) from narrative inquiry, a methodology? They explain narrative inquiry as "a methodology that takes stories, as they appear or are constructed from a variety of experiences and artifacts, as the unit of analysis for understanding relational aspects of human experience" (Sisk-Hilton & Meier, 2016, p. 7).

Within a context that deprofessionalizes teachers and seeks to position us as technicians (Giroux, 1988), the stories and examples shared in this book invite us to reclaim the role of teachers as researchers, not apart from teaching, but (re)positioning research centrally. Daniel and Stephanie "emphasize the power of narrative inquiry for observing student learning and engagement, reflecting on one's teaching philosophies and practices, promoting teacher agency and voice, and creating transformative communities" (Sisk-Hilton & Meier, 2016, p. 14). They argue that we need teachers' voices in educational research and that narrative inquiry—as they propose, describe, and exemplify—can possibilitate just that.

In making narrative inquiry accessible, Daniel and Stephanie define the foundational tenets of narrative inquiry as well as its connections to practice, and links to its content standards. They elucidate the value and affordances of narrative inquiry for professional growth and development. Yet, they recognize that micro narratives are positioned within the context of macro narratives (Souto-Manning, 2014a; 2014b), which inform structural conditions and available resources for fostering equity and justice for the children they teach along with their families and communities—and for us as teachers.

As an historical construction, curriculum and teaching are micro narratives historically and sociopolitically shaped by macro narratives (Souto-Manning, 2014a; 2014b). These macro narratives privilege some ways of knowing while marginalizing and minoritizing others. In dominant ways of teaching and in dominant curricula, the narratives and ways with words of minoritized individuals and groups are often silenced, left out, or purposefully excluded. Today, the term "minority" is often numerically inaccurate. As McCarty (2002) explained: "'Minoritized' more accurately conveys the power relations and processes by which certain groups are socially, economically, and politically marginalized within the larger society. The term also implies human agency" (p. xv).

Daniel and Stephanie invite us to recognize how children's storytelling reveals children's use of language, understanding of concepts, and learning of strategies within the context of their cultural practices and values (Delgado-Gaitan & Trueba, 1991), unveiling their potentialities. Further, they position narrative inquiry as a tool to challenge what is the current landscape of teaching, which is framed by dominant values and ideals. From their perspective, narrative inquiry can foster teacher-student collaborations, (re)positioning students as co-researchers who engage in collective counter-storytelling (Solórzano & Yosso, 2002), fostering spaces of "transformative resistance" (Solórzano & Delgado Bernal, 2001).

Daniel and Stephanie invite us teachers to (re)claim narratives as ways of teaching, assessing, searching, and researching. They invite us to inquire; to ask questions. To carefully consider "puzzling moments" (Ballenger, 2009); they show us how narrative inquiry is a puzzle. They invite us to write down our observations, to document our journey and the journeys of the children in our classrooms—individually and collectively. And then to reread and interpret their meanings; to recognize, envision, and realize the ways in which narratives reveal much more than "objective data." Through rich examples, Daniel and Stephanie invite us to revision our teaching based on narrative inquiry grounded in the actions and interactions of young children.

Daniel and Stephanie remind us of the power of listening, learning, and documenting children's journeys as they develop as individuals and as members of a community. They urge us to embrace the power and possibility of narrative inquiry to foster transformative teaching. They call us to engage in narrative inquiry to transform education. They urge us to expand what we have come to regard as research, with a step-by-step procedure going from problem to solution via questioning and inquiry. They reaffirm the focus of narrative inquiry on "a particular wonder" (Clandinin & Connelly, 2000, p. 24) or "puzzling moment" (Ballenger,

2009). Daniel and Stephanie invite us to inquire into the storylines created in our classrooms, seeking to understand the relationships and understandings children negotiate and develop. They open windows into narrative inquiries in a variety of settings using myriad tools.

At a time in which children are being urged to progress faster and faster, racing toward mastering standards (Genishi & Dyson, 2012), "narrative inquiry takes a step back from our rush to fix things, instead requiring us to understand the intertwined and complex stories that are embodied in the people who inhabit our classrooms" (Sisk-Hilton & Meier, 2016, p. 37). Narrative inquiry affords us the space to document children's assets—what they *can* do. It allows us to reorganize the classroom and its learning spaces, shifting the focus from remediating students to re-mediating (Gutiérrez, Morales, & Martínez, 2009) children's learning experiences. Instead of emphasizing basic skills—problems of the individual—re-mediation involves a reorganization of the entire ecology for learning" (p. 227). It allows us the space to understand the meanings and intentions behind their practices—instead of hurrying to judge them against a set standard or norm (which often excludes, segregates, and marginalizes).

Narrative inquiry—as explained and proposed by Daniel and Stephanie—afford us the time, space, and impetus for envisioning a pedagogy of possibility which honors students multiple storylines and learning trajectories. They remind us that narrative inquiry can foster intentional, purposeful, and ongoing reflection and self-study. It can help us consider multiple perspectives and varying points of view. It acknowledges the danger of what Adichie (2009) called "single stories" in teaching and learning. It results in improved practices and leads to curricular reforms that center on the needs, practices, and priorities of young children.

As you turn the page and start reading this book, I invite you to reflect on how narrative inquiry can inform your teaching and transform you as a teacher. I invite you to inquire alongside Daniel, Stephanie, and the many teacher-researchers whose stories are portrayed in this book. I urge you to identify a persistent problem, to get in the habit of collecting and composing narratives about your teaching, and to author your stories of practice. And as you engage in a new learning journey as a narrative inquirer or deepen your practice as a teacher-researcher, remember: "Never give up. There is no such thing as an ending. Just a new beginning" (Maya Angelou).

We teachers hold incredible power. We are privileged to be privy to the multiple storylines children negotiate and the many narratives they (co)author each day, having access to small glimpses into the stories that shape who we are and who our students are becoming. In multiple ways—through collages, observational notes, journals and diaries, letters, and drama—may we use this power to transform education in more hopeful, humane, and powerful ways. After all, narrative inquiry has the potential to foster new beginnings—not only for us as teachers, but for the children we teach—because "stories are never 'finished'" (Sisk-Hilton & Meier, 2016, p. 61).

Mariana Souto-Manning, Teachers College, Columbia University

References

Adichie, C. (2009). *The danger of a single story*. Retrieved on June 6, 2016 from www.ted
.com/talks/chimamanda_adichie_the_danger_of_a_single_story?language=en.

Ballenger, C. (2009). *Puzzling moments, teachable moments: Practicing teacher research in urban
classrooms*. New York, NY: Teachers College Press.

Clandinin, D. J., & Connelly, F. M. (2000). *Narrative inquiry: Experience and story in qualitative
research*. San Francisco, CA: Jossey-Bass.

Delgado-Gaitan, C., & Trueba, H. (1999). *Crossing cultural borders: Education for immigrant
families in America*. London, UK: Falmer Press.

Genishi, C., & Dyson, A. Haas. (2012). Racing to the top: Who's accounting for the children? *Bank Street Occasional Papers, 27*, 18–20.

Giroux, H. (1988). *Teachers as intellectuals: Toward a critical pedagogy of learning*. Westport, CT:
Bergin & Garvey.

Gutiérrez, K., Morales, P., & Martínez, D. (2009). Re-mediating literacy: Culture, difference, and learning for students from nondominant communities. *Review of Research in
Education, 33*, 212–245.

Ladson-Billings, G. (1995). But that's just good teaching! The case for culturally relevant
pedagogy. *Theory into Practice 34*(3), 159–165.

McCarty, T. (2002). *A place to be Navajo: Rough Rock and the struggle for self-determination in
Indigenous schooling*. New York, NY: Routledge.

Ochs, E., Smith, R., & Taylor, C. (1996). Detective stories at dinnertime: Problem solving through co-narration. In C. Briggs (Ed.), *Disorderly discourse: Narrative, conflict, and
inequality* (pp. 95–113). New York, NY: Oxford University Press.

Paley, V. G. (1990). *The boy who would be a helicopter: The uses of storytelling in the classroom*.
Cambridge, MA: Harvard University Press.

Sisk-Hilton, S., & Meier, D. (2016). *Narrative inquiry in early childhood and elementary school:
Learning to teach, teaching well*. New York, NY: Routledge.

Solórzano, D., & Delgado Bernal, D. (2001). Examining transformational critical race and
Latcrit theory framework: Chicana and Chicano students in an urban context. *Urban
Education, 36*(3), 308–342.

Solórzano, D., & Yosso, T. (2002). Critical race methodology: Counter-storytelling as an
analytical framework for education research. *Qualitative Inquiry, 8*(1), 23–44.

Souto-Manning, M. (2014a). Critical narrative analysis: The interplay of critical discourse
and narrative analyses. *International Journal of Qualitative Studies in Education, 27*(2),
159–180.

Souto-Manning, M. (2014b). Critical for whom?: Theoretical and methodological dilemmas in critical approaches to language research. In D. Paris & M. Winn
(Eds.), *Humanizing research: Decolonizing qualitative inquiry with youth and communities*
(pp. 201–222). Thousand Oaks, CA: SAGE.

Souto-Manning, M., & Martell, J. (2016). *Reading, writing, and talk: Inclusive teaching strategies
for diverse learners, K–2*. New York, NY: Teachers College Press.

ACKNOWLEDGMENTS

Daniel wishes to acknowledge and thank Stephanie for her creative and dedicated work on this project, which has allowed me a new place for contributing my ideas and work in the area of narrative inquiry. Stephanie would like to thank Daniel for his tireless work to bring narrative inquiry into the lives of teachers and the vast knowledge and enthusiasm he brought to this project. We also thank the teachers who gave of themselves and their teaching to add their contributions to this volume—Emily Starr Bean, Kathie Behlen, Rachel Castro, Michael Escamilla, Bob Garrison, Nicole Ginocchio, Alina Gish, Renetta Goeson, Sophia Jimenez, Martha Melgoza, Kirsti Jewel Peters-Hoyte, and Andrea Pierotti. We also thank the children featured in this book for their joyful learning and great stories of development and achievement, and Barbara Henderson and Maria Zavala for their reviews of the manuscript. Thanks also go to Dr. Mariana Souto-Manning for her insightful foreword and affirmation of the book's goals and value. Final thanks to the great Routledge editorial team of Alex Masulis, Senior Editor, and Daniel Schwartz, Senior Editorial Assistant.

INTRODUCTION

Maybe stories are just data with a soul.

Brené Brown

Storytelling is part of every human society. It appears that our brains are hardwired to attend to stories in ways fundamentally different than the ways in which we process other forms of input (Willingham, 2004). Teachers of young children know this through experience, as does anyone who has ever sat and read a story with a child or recounted a memory of one's own childhood to the delight of a young audience. Stories convey important elements of our cultures and worldviews. They instruct us, transmit values, and offer warnings that often serve to create boundaries and also bridges within and between cultures. Stories have power in part because they are remembered. And yet our memories are tricky vessels, not encapsulating lived experience with complete fidelity, but rather massaging and changing experiences into stories that help us define who we are, who we are not, and how we relate to the world around us.

How then, can ever-changing, imperfectly remembered, fundamentally subjective stories become a form of research and improving practice? In much of modern schooling, we have been taught that story and research are, in fact, entirely different things. Research, after all, is the search for truth, quantifiable and reproducible results that answer core questions and puzzles: How is information transmitted and processed in the brain? How did humans evolve from single celled life forms? How can we remove carbon from the atmosphere and put it back into the earth's surface? And yet, even within scientific inquiry, there are elements of stories and storytelling. For instance, understanding natural selection involves engaging with and building a narrative of how an organism interacts with its environment and engages in selective reproduction over multiple generations: the story of a species. Further, stories and narrative hold together and build communities of practice over time. Donald Braid (2006), in analyzing the role of storytelling among physicists, discusses the power of story as a means of instruction, coherence building, and thought experimentation. He explains:

> I believe that physicists tell oral stories because they provide an important vehicle for teaching elusive strategies for doing good physics that cannot be taught through formal theory, text books, or teaching methods. The key to understanding how stories provide a unique teaching medium lies in understanding that listeners do not passively absorb storytelling performances . . . The listener must follow the story as it unfolds, trying to integrate the emerging information into a coherent sense of "what happened" in the event being narrated. Because the coherence-making that takes place when one follows a story parallels the coherence-making that takes place in direct experiencing, listeners can explore the words and actions of the narrated event similarly to how they explore their own lived experiences. (p. 154)

As Braid's research reveals, there is a rich history of narrative as a form of meaning making even within the so-called "hard sciences." The field of *narrative inquiry*, as distinguished from mere use of narrative, has developed as a methodology that takes stories, as they appear or are constructed from a variety of experiences and artifacts, as the unit of analysis for understanding relational aspects of human experience across a wide variety of disciplines. There is a rich history of narrative inquiry in the fields of medicine, women's studies, psychology, and anthropology, as well as in educational research. In all of these fields, there is a need to understand how individuals and groups construct meaning, and this requires considering the stories of participants' experiences in and out of the settings that researchers are studying. In order to understand how a child thinks about how plants grow, we need to know the story of her planting herbs with her grandmother, the story of her noticing weeds pushing up through the sidewalk near her high-rise apartment building, the story of her picking a dandelion and watching it wilt, not knowing how to bring it back to life. Likewise, to understand a teacher's impatience with a disruptive child, the teacher himself might reach back to retrieve the story of his own childhood, how children were expected to behave in the classrooms of his memory, how adults who could not "control" children were judged, and perhaps the punishment that he endured when he spoke out of turn or brought playground energy into the classroom.

Our brains automatically seek meaning in stories. What *narrative inquiry for teaching* adds is an invitation for teachers to seek out stories that inform a particular puzzle or problem of practice, to develop ways to analyze for multiple meanings and explanations, to make the collection and consideration of narratives an integral part of learning to teach and teaching well. In this book, we explore what it means for teachers to engage in narrative inquiry not just for the purpose of completing a single research project, but rather as a stance toward the teaching and learning process that can inform practice in a transformative and ongoing way.

Why Engage in Narrative Inquiry for Teaching?

Often, teachers' first exposure to narrative inquiry is during their graduate studies. They may be drawn to narrative inquiry as it connects to the daily life of their classroom, to the goal they likely already have of understanding of complex lives of their students. But too often, we believe, narrative inquiry, like many other forms of research, remains housed in the walls of academia. When teachers are done with graduate school and return full time to the classroom, they are thrown back into a world that demands instant reaction to hundreds of inputs, demands, and expectations every day. In this book, we offer a view of narrative inquiry *for* teaching, rather than narrative inquiry *about* teaching. We propose the narrative inquiry approach as a way of being in and learning with a community of learners, as a critical part of teaching practice. We hope that the examples and methodologies provided here show how narrative inquiry can become a core part of teachers' daily lives and work, one that feeds them and aids their professional growth.

We also argue for the importance of narrative inquiry for teaching at the level of policy and knowledge building within the larger field of education. The voices of teachers are too little represented in the educational research literature. In order to truly understand the complex world of classrooms, we desperately need the perspectives and insights of teachers. Narrative inquiry allows teachers to examine what matters in their setting, with the children in their classroom, but it also presents the opportunity for teachers' knowledge and understanding to be shared more publicly and for us to better learn from each other. As a field, we need teachers' voices to inform educational research, and the model of narrative inquiry for teaching outlined here is a way forward toward this goal.

Dimensions of Narrative Inquiry for Teaching

In the chapters that follow, we address three dimensions of teachers' narrative inquiry that are critical to making narrative inquiry methodology part of one's teaching practice rather than an activity that stands apart from the teaching and learning process. First, we define *narrative inquiry as research*. This may seem the most obvious of statements given the subject of the book, but in schools and educational systems dominated by a focus on quantitative data, it is important to state at the outset that we propose narrative inquiry as a research methodology particularly well-suited to building understanding of teaching and learning in classrooms. When teachers begin the process of narrative inquiry, they sometimes feel as though they are "just telling stories." And in fact, that may be a necessary first step, as stories are a valuable way to capture and process the complex activities of the classroom. But narrative *inquiry* moves beyond storytelling, gathering narratives in a methodical way, using analytical tools and lenses to find meaning, and deliberately seeking counter-narratives to examine specific puzzles and problems of teaching. Chapter 1 describes key aspects of narrative inquiry as research, and Chapter 3 explores tools and methods for collecting and analyzing narrative data for teaching.

Second, we propose that narrative inquiry for teaching is *necessarily linked to children's learning*. Narrative inquiry, with its grounding in the collection and analysis of stories, focuses on the relational aspects of the classroom. As teachers seek to understand multiple aspects of children's lives and experiences in and out of the classroom, they gain a better understanding of the factors that facilitate, challenge, and contextualize learning. We argue that this depth of understanding is an important means of improving teachers' abilities to adjust curriculum, lessons, and classroom structures to improve both the learning experience and ultimately, learning outcomes, for their students. Chapter 2 describes the power of narrative as a tool to identify and explore puzzles and problems of practice that are sometimes hidden in more narrow forms of data collection, and in this chapter we also discuss the importance of seeking counter-narratives to avoid using research as a means of simply confirming what we believe to be true. Chapter 4 examines specific ways in which teachers go about collecting and analyzing stories of children's experiences.

Finally, this book embraces the idea of *narrative inquiry for the purpose of educational change*. Teachers often have an understandable impatience for the field of educational research when the results do not have clear and immediate applications for their classrooms. As educational researchers ourselves, we would gently argue that often, exploratory research without immediate pragmatic application is necessary to expand our understanding of children's learning. However, as we are also teachers working with children, we understand the impatience and know that what classroom teachers need today, next week, and next year, is a way to engage in research that has clear meaning and application in their specific teaching setting. We approach narrative inquiry for teaching as a methodology in which teachers, often in conjunction with their students, define the puzzles and problems that are most important to their teaching setting. We encourage teachers to take up narrative inquiry as a means of examining what confuses them about a child, what troubles them in their daily practice, what keeps them up at night. Narrative inquiry does not generally lead to a quick and simple "fix" of a persistent problem, but the exploration and search for understanding can be a powerful means of educational change. Chapter 6 takes up ways in which teachers may engage in narrative inquiry around areas of language and literacy, and Chapter 7 presents a "whole" example of one teacher's narrative inquiry project to demonstrate how this approach of methodical story collection, reflection, and analysis may lead to change.

A Note About the Authors and the Many Contributors to This Work

The examples we use in this book draw from the authors' wide range of experience both engaging in narrative inquiry in our own research and in supporting narrative inquiry–based work with teachers in early childhood and elementary settings. Both of us have backgrounds as classroom teachers, Daniel as a preschool and kindergarten teacher and Stephanie as an elementary and middle school teacher. Daniel engages in narrative inquiry around children's language and literacy development. In addition, he works with early childhood educators engaged in graduate studies and in inquiry work at school sites throughout the San Francisco Bay Area and worldwide. Many of the examples of narrative inquiry in this book come from teachers who have developed narrative inquiry for teaching in conjunction with Daniel over the years as part of the San Francisco State University MA program in Early Childhood Education. In addition, Daniel's ongoing partnership with the educators at Las Americas Preschool in San Francisco shows the power of narrative inquiry as a way of life for a group of teachers, and we draw widely upon the work of these educators.

Stephanie has long been drawn to story, and spent the first part of her life wanting to be a fiction writer. As a classroom teacher, she collected voluminous narratives from herself and her students and always suspected that the accumulated journals were the main way she learned to be a better teacher, despite having no real method behind her approach. However, when she began graduate school in cognition and development, she temporarily put away that part of herself, focused on mastering the more standard methodologies of educational research. She circled back to story only later, when she discovered that an entire methodology existed called narrative inquiry! Most of her research falls into the field of first-person teacher research, and so she maintains an active teaching practice in elementary schools. She uses narrative inquiry as one of several methodologies for analyzing her teaching practice, so many of the examples throughout this book come from her work as an elementary teacher and researcher. In addition, two of her former graduate students have graciously allowed their work in narrative inquiry to be featured here.

Of course, narrative inquiry for teaching means narrative inquiry about, and often with, children. Throughout the book, excerpts from teachers' narrative inquiries include stories of children, and often children's own words and pictures are included. To protect the privacy of these young people, we have changed their names. In addition, adults who appear in narrative segments in the role of students but not co-inquirers (see Chapter 4) are named with pseudonyms, with key identifying features left out. Teachers whose work appears throughout the book are named and given full credit. This system seeks to both honor the important work of narrative inquiry for teaching and protect potentially vulnerable populations who cannot yet give their full consent to share their stories.

This book is not only co-written, but also draws upon the voices and experiences of a large number of teacher researcher colleagues. These contributors present findings from their own individual research projects as well as those of many others in early childhood and elementary classrooms across the country. In order to aid the reader in keeping track of individual narratives, we have chosen to use the names of the co-authors, Daniel and Stephanie, as appropriate throughout the body of the text. The exception to this is in the samples of narrative research that appear in each chapter. In these, we have kept the first person "I" when the narrative was originally written that way and noted the author at the beginning of the segment. Additionally, because both Daniel and Stephanie identify as teachers who engage in narrative inquiry, the term "we" is often used to refer more broadly to the community of U.S. teachers, of which we are a part.

1

WHY NARRATIVE INQUIRY?

In this chapter we discuss particular forms and functions of narrative inquiry for teaching and learning from early childhood through elementary school. We emphasize the power of narrative inquiry for observing student learning and engagement; reflecting on one's teaching philosophies and practices; promoting teacher agency and voice; and creating transformative communities of teachers, students, and families. In doing so, we discuss the place of narrative inquiry in educational research, basic tenets of narrative inquiry, connections to practice, links to content standards, and the value of narrative inquiry for professional growth and development. We intend this opening chapter as a foundational piece for the rest of the book, and invite you to begin your own narrative inquiry story here. You might ask yourself the following questions as you read and consider the connections to your teaching and professional work: How do I value story in my daily life? In my professional life? What stories are central to my personal and professional identity and to my practice? How might stories as combined with an inquiry stance toward teaching and learning improve my work? Where might I start in my work to include elements of narrative inquiry?

What is Narrative Inquiry?

Narrative inquiry is a subset of qualitative research, and has a large extended family of "research cousins"—teacher research and inquiry (Cochran-Smith & Lytle, 2009; Hubbard & Power, 2003; Meier & Henderson, 2007; Zeichner & Liston, 2014), self-study and inquiry (Kroll, 2012; Strong-Wilson, 2006), action research (Pushor & Clandinin, 2009), arts-based approaches to research (Eisner & Barone, 2011), the qualitative approach of portraiture (Lawrence-Lightfoot & Davis, 1997; Lawrence-Lightfoot, 2005), life histories in medicine (Coles, 1990) and in psychotherapy (Speedy, 2008), narrative-based essays (hooks, 2008), case studies (Merriam, 1988), phenomenological interviewing (Seidman, 2013), narrative-based poetry as research (Boylorn, 2011), autobiography and fiction (Bold, 2012), auto-ethnography (Jones, 1998), and anthropological accounts and field notes (Geertz, 1988). All of these approaches make use of narrative accounts in different ways, as part of the research process. However, what makes narrative inquiry for teaching distinct from these related methodologies is the reliance on *narrative as the unit of analysis* for identifying and examining issues of teaching and learning. That is, the stories collected directly or constructed from artifacts of children's and teachers' experiences in and out of the class-room become the dataset that the teacher researcher analyzes for meaning, for existence of counter-narratives, and for ways to address ongoing puzzles and problems of practice.

Narrative inquiry has gained increasing attention as a methodology or approach in educational research for promoting teacher knowledge of student learning, effective instructional practices, and teacher agency and professional growth. Narrative has been shown to strengthen the voice of researchers, uncover and chronicle life histories and critical events, and connect the personal and professional lives of participants in educational settings (Barone, 2001; Clandinin & Connelly, 2000; Clandinin, 2013; Connelly & Clandinin, 1990; Coulter & Smith, 2009; Lyons & LaBoskey, 2002; Pagnucci, 2004; Riessman, 2008). Proponents of narrative inquiry and story have pointed their lenses at a host of critical issues and topics in teaching, learning, and schooling—child development (Edwards & Rinaldi, 2009), children's play (Paley, 1981), language and literacy education (Goswami, Lewis, Rutherford, & Waff, 2009), racism and social justice (Bell & Roberts, 2010; Diaz Soto, 2008; Winn, 2010, 2011), notions of special needs and identity (Valente, 2011), invisibility and recognition in educational institutions (Reddick & Saénz, 2012), immigrant teachers (Elbaz-Luwisch, 2004), and trauma and resilience in childhood (Wright, 2010). In a fundamental way, narrative inquiry relies on particular forms and functions of narrative for understanding experience and constructing reality (Bruner, 1991; Hardy, 1977), for human creativity and imagination (Egan, 1986, 1992), and for social and educational change (Freire, 1967/1976; Gadotti & Torres, 2009).

Looking broadly on a global scale, narrative inquiry has the potential to strengthen local practices in international contexts and to promote the exchange of professional stories across geographic, cultural, philosophical, and political boundaries. Many cultures and educational practices place profound importance on story as ensuring cultural continuity, moral development, and social cohesion. In numerous international contexts, for instance, religious texts and teachings rely on story as a primary vehicle for moral and religious teaching and observance. In cultures and traditions that emphasize oral traditions, story is central to one's worldview and to one's relationship to self and others and notions of time, development, and learning.

In early childhood education, the Reggio Emilia educators in Northern Italy have garnered international interest in their approach to teaching that features multiple linguistic modes of learning and the use of narrative as a foundation for documentation (Edwards & Rinaldi, 2009; Edwards, Gandini, & Forman, 2012). Educators in New Zealand (Pohio, Sansom, & Liley, 2015) believe in the power of narrative for creating engaging curriculum for young children that features storytelling by adults and children, and the use of teacher reflection and documentation that affirms the bicultural and bilingual identities of children and adults within the teaching-learning process. Japan makes use of lesson study (Lewis & Tsuchida, 1998) that emphasizes the exchange of stories, key incidents, and insights between teaching colleagues within and amongst more than one school. Finland's preservice and inservice teacher education (Sahlberg, 2014) places a premium on the intellectual exchange of information and insights into one's teaching and that of others. This exchange and dialogue is designed to promote teachers as inquisitive lifelong learners who work in an environment of trust and the general Finnish professional milieu of teachers as foundations for a democratic and ethical society. While the approaches above would not necessarily be classified as *research through narrative inquiry* in that they do not always engage in analysis of story or narrative, all show the compelling nature of story to document, consider, and exchange ideas about teaching and learning.

Narrative inquiry, though, is not without its detractors, who point to the problematic aspects of narrative regarding the trustworthiness and rigor of narrative-based data, its objectivity and distance from one's bias and individual perspectives, and its purported lack of generalizability to disparate participants and contexts. However, we acknowledge that there is bias in every form of research, in terms of what is chosen as the topic of study, what features the researchers attend to, and who or what serve as subjects of study versus creators of knowledge. For those who approach narrative inquiry for teaching as a way of examining their own practice, accessing one's own stories and deliberately seeking out those of others often makes clear that our judgments about students and the learning environment are, in fact, just that—judgments, not "objective" assessments of the way things are. As the authors of this book, we show the power of narrative inquiry to take on relational aspects of teaching and learning that are often obscured by other research methodologies but which are critical to how teachers and learners operate within classrooms and beyond. While we are interested in addressing some of the problematic aspects of narrative inquiry, we primarily want to describe and show how narrative inquiry can be a positive force for improving student achievement and empowering teachers across the early childhood and elementary school continuum. We emphasize, then, several key elements of narrative inquiry that we argue are central for the linking of "*points of inquiry*" with "*points of practice*" that lead to "*points of educational change.*"

We define narrative inquiry as the valuing of story as a way of life, as a way of remembering, as a form of educational research, and as a way to understand and improve our educational practice. Our stories come in many forms—oral, written, drawn, photographed, dramatized—and are essential to improving teaching and educational transformation. Teacher narrative inquiry embraces the collection and analysis of stories as a means to examine puzzles of practice through the lens of understanding and unpacking relational elements and participants' lived experiences in and out of the classroom. Narrative inquiry moves beyond a single story to purposefully identify counter-narratives to understand and transform the complexity of classroom life.

Memoir, Memory, and Identity

Well-told stories that resonate with us personally and professionally are often linked to our lived experiences, feelings, thoughts, hopes, and dreams. They connect with us because they touch critical aspects of who we are as members of social and cultural communities with particular values, beliefs, and practices (Loseke, 2007). The stories that touch us exist internally (in our mind and heart and soul as internal monologue) and externally (in our actions, talk, movements as external dialogue with objects and others), and pertain to what matters most to our success as educators and as professionals.

> We view the landscape as narratively constructed: as having a history with moral, emotional, and aesthetic dimensions. We see it as storied. To enter a professional knowledge landscape is to enter a place of story. The landscape is composed of two fundamentally different places, the in-classroom place and the out-of-classroom place. (Clandinin & Connelly, 1999, p. 2)

In the course of our professional growth, wherever we might be on the novice to veteran span, we carry with us an accumulated deposit of valuable observations and insights into our teaching and our own learning. We catalogue, whether consciously or not, a myriad of moments, vignettes, events, objects, and interactions that we sort and filter as we teach and learn and grow. We tend to remember those details of feeling and thought and action that matter to us, that impinge upon our professional philosophies, interests, goals, and practices. In essence, the accumulation of these memories helps form our identities as individuals and as professionals, providing us with our foundational interests, strengths, and areas of educational expertise.

Much of the power of narrative inquiry, as linked to memoir and memory, is predicated on the value of remembering, of reliving and re-seeing. As the writer Garrett Hongo (1995) wrote in his memoir, "An old story, deep in my memory, had emerged out of the fogs and into the light. I must have heard it dozens of times during my childhood. My mother would speak it like a myth or a fable . . . " The process of narrative inquiry enables us to "re-vision our narratives" (Strong-Wilson, 2006), and as we engage with our own narratives and others', educators are "more likely to commit" to "reflecting on the implications of those [narrative-based] constructions for practice" (p. 61). Much of our "success" with narrative inquiry in educational contexts is predicated on our openness to embracing our memories and those critical events, experiences, ideas, and feelings that intertwine our personal and professional lives, as well as our openness to counter-narratives, the stories of others that may interpret events and actions completely differently than we do. As we ponder a particular teaching and learning puzzle in a deep way, more often than not, the process of going back in time to revisit an event or idea impinges upon our memories. There are two critical forms of memory that narrative inquirers touch upon—episodic, which refers to those events or experiences that happened at a particular place and time, and semantic, referring to events and experiences that continue and evolve, and are not associated with specific times or places (Engel, 1999). For instance, we might puzzle over a particular series of events that occur during a particular classroom routine at a certain time each day, which would involve elements of episodic memory. We might also puzzle over a recurring feeling or idea that has accumulated over time, which would involve elements of semantic memory. Often, in narrative inquiry journeys, there is a combination of both forms of memory.

Wrestling with our personal and professional memories around a particular teaching and learning puzzle often takes us on an unexpected journey of remembering, reflecting, and changing. As Engel (1999) notes, "Every memory journeys from its first vivid moment within a person to its multifarious transformations and uses within the world" (p. 3). And when we engage in narrative inquiry with others at school sites and beyond, our memories further evolve—"When a memory takes a public form it doesn't necessarily lose its internal psychological intensity, but it may subtly transform it . . . Sometimes the public use of a memory gives it a definition and substance it didn't have when it lived only in one's mind as a fleeting and infrequent visitor" (p. 16).

The narrative inquiry process of remembering, reliving, and reflecting also has implications for changes in our identities as educators and as narrative inquirers. Looking for and finding particular memories of certain children, actions, ideas, strategies, or materials in our memory banks complicates the narrative plotlines of who we are as educators. The narrative theorist Paul Ricouer (1988) wrote,

> In the first place, narrative identity is not a stable and seamless identity. Just as it is possible to compose several plots on the same subject of the same incidents (which, thus, should not really be called the same events), so it is always possible to weave different, even opposed, plots about our lives. (p. 248)

The process of remembering critical stories helps us see multiple storylines and plotlines for teaching that complicate our narrative inquiries, and thus deepens our identities as richly textured educators. Part of this deepening of our identities can bring about a more prominent role for imagination in our work lives—"Our analysis of the act of reading leads us to say rather that the practice of narrative lies in a thought experiment by means of which we try to inhabit the worlds foreign to us" (Ricouer, 1988, p. 249). The process of engaging with narrative, of looking into our memories, can thus bring about new possibilities for identity formation as educators.

Macro and Micro Narratives

The art of teaching and learning is essentially the continual unfolding of the small *micro* level narratives enacted between children, teachers, families—all the micro interactions and activities of classroom life—that are set against (sometimes in happy concert, sometimes in conflict) the larger, *macro* stories of institutional and professional traditions, expectations, and power structures. While we live and work within the covert and overt parameters of these larger macro narratives, narrative inquiry encompasses and helps us integrate the range of small and large narratives that influence our teaching lives, and the trajectory of our teaching over time (Clandinin, 2013; Souto-Manning & Ray, 2007).

The macro narratives, by and large, influence the structures and resources for teachers to maximize equity and social justice for teachers, children, and their families. These larger, all-encompassing narratives are the grand, dominant narratives (Polkinghorne, 1988) that dominate the discourse on a particular approach to schooling, teaching, assessment, and reform. They constitute the larger realities of classroom life and teaching that impinge upon the teacher-student relationship, and largely determine the potential for professional growth and change outside of one's classroom. The narratives, though, that matter most to teachers within the classroom, link one's personal and professional lives, and help us understand and deepen our educational philosophies, curriculum, instructional practices, and human relationships.

In his last interview, Paulo Freire (1996) argued for questioning "the dominant syntax" in education and teaching—to reflect and act in opposition to those social, cultural, historical, and educational forces that exclude silent and marginalized individuals, groups, and communities. To reclaim a more rightful and just position in education and society, narrative inquiry looks at the role of counter-narratives and counter-storytelling (Witherell, 2004), placing of texts in juxtaposition to each other (Fischer, 1986; Strong-Wilson, 2006), and *testimonios* (Delgado, 1989) to challenge the prevailing grand narratives and the "dominant syntax." These transformative stories have the potential to alter one's thinking, promote the potential for action, and begin to chip away or even break long-standing views and ideas that influence our teaching and children's learning. For instance, counter-stories can break down stereotypes promoted by the media and popular culture (Myers, 2013), views on the linguistic and cognitive capabilities of children and adults who are said to speak "broken English" (Tan, 1990), and the language and framing of an "achievement gap" as continuing a deficit view of children of Color (Ladson-Billings, 2007). The counter-stories of teachers and children can create a new kind of space and way of thinking and feeling that nibbles away at the dominant syntax. Narrative inquiry also can provide a framework for teachers and students to collaborate and become co-researchers, co-thinkers, and co-storytellers (Lewis, 2009) and to break down traditional barriers between teacher and student.

Narrative Inquiry as a Puzzle

Narrative inquiry, in contrast with more traditional modes of educational inquiry, does not advocate a problem–question–hypothesis–solution paradigm or cycle, but rather the view of narrative inquiry as "always composed around a particular wonder, a research puzzle" (Clandinin & Connelly, 2000, p. 124). These "puzzling moments" (Ballenger, 2009) might entail looking at an aspect of successful classroom teaching and exploring the underlying reasons for the success. Or we might be puzzled by a recurring or recent aspect of teaching that is an impediment to more effective instruction or personal relationships in the classroom. The puzzle might focus on an aspect of curriculum, a particular child, a teaching strategy or set of strategies, the classroom environment, or human relationships. The puzzle and the beginnings of narrative inquiry work provide the spark, the intellectual and emotional and even political push toward looking more deeply at what might be going on beneath the surface of classroom teaching and life. There is a range of possible *prompts* or story starters for embarking on a narrative inquiry journey:

- Puzzles ("I wonder why none of the girls ever play in the block corner.")
- Predicaments ("I continue to provide one-on-one support for a certain student in reading, but she sometimes forgets the sight words and basic decoding strategies that I just taught her the day before.")
- Unexplained successes ("All of the children in the class are playing so well this year outside, and there are so few arguments. I wonder why?")
- An immediate need for change and intervention! ("One child continues to bite another child and the parents are calling me daily . . .")
- Noticings ("I notice that the editing partners in writers workshop are finally clicking this month. I haven't changed the routine, and so I wonder why . . .")
- Empowerment and agency ("I need to find a stronger voice in staff meetings and within my teaching team . . .")
- Politics and power ("I am committed to social justice and equity around access to content knowledge, and I am interested in improving the access of girls in my class to participation and discussion during science.")

Narrative inquirers can look for possible new plotlines from an initial puzzle by examining specific aspects of classroom environments, materials, curriculum, teaching practices, children's conversations, student work and play samples, and student ideas and feelings.

Documentation

A well-told story often captures the journey over a certain period of time. Along the way, narrative inquirers document key elements of a project or series of activities by focusing on critical aspects of setting, events, characters, materials, products, and reflections. This process of documentation can take focus on a range of data sources through varied narrative inquiry tools (Edwards, Gandini, & Forman, 2012; Kastle, 2012; Perry, Henderson, & Meier, 2012). For instance, as we discuss in Chapter 3, elements of teaching and learning can be documented—in the form of observational notes or teaching journal, the collection of children's work and play samples, audiotaping of conversation and talk, photographs of children at work and play, video recordings that capture visuals and sound, informal conversations, more formal interviews, and surveys and questionnaires. In an attempt to capture an unfolding story in real time, documentation can also occur *in the midst of teaching*. In this process, narrative inquirers write down brief notes on sticky notes or a small pad of paper kept in a pocket, snippets of action and talk are captured via a cell phone or iPad, collect work and play samples, and enlist one's colleagues, and even the children as co-researchers to collect data. Later, when time and space and energy allows, the collected material can be organized, catalogued, and reflected upon.

Still later, particular material or data can be selected to analyze in a more fine-grained manner, highlighting only small aspects or elements from an activity, lesson, incident, conversation, or project that illuminate key discoveries and lessons learned from the initial inquiry puzzle. The results of this distillation process can be captured and presented in a range of narrative inquiry products for public dissemination and sharing with children, colleagues, and families. These products can take the form of *documentation* panels or documentation books (usually made of paper of various sizes) consisting of teachers' observational and interpretive text, photographs of the children and adults at work and play, and selected work and play samples from the children (Given, Kuh, LeeKeenan, Mardell, Redditt, & Twombly, 2010; Meier & Henderson, 2007). Documentation can also take the form of informal sharing of chosen student products with colleagues or families via conversation, or multimedia presentation through PowerPoint, Prezi, email, blog, Facebook, or iMovie. The multimedia forms of documentation can be private for a particular group or made more public, for "open" audiences. Forms of documentation may be kept by narrative inquirers for short or long periods of time, and the multimedia forms have the distinct advantage of saving physical space for storage and future retrieval.

What Does Narrative Reveal About Teaching? An Example from Practice

In the past decade, the amount of data that teachers are expected to analyze about their students and about their teaching has increased at a phenomenal rate. It is not unusual to see graphs and tables of student performance over time in classrooms, school offices, and even hallways, sometimes posted prominently for everyone to examine. Faculty meetings and teacher collaboration time are often spent examining results of benchmark assessments, looking for trends in data and areas that need improvement.

This rise in "data-driven" education certainly has some positive aspects. Knowing with some precision each student's areas of mastery and struggle can help teachers design lessons tailored to specific needs. A focus on quantitative data can also reveal what we have not yet measured well, areas on which we are relying too much on intuition and general impressions, sometimes under- or overestimating children's level of understanding. And formal, quantitative assessments tend to be given to every child. While the idea that a single, formal assessment can measure each child equally troubles many of us who spend time in classrooms, the rise of data-driven education has ensured that we do, in fact, have some sort of data to consider for every child in a classroom. As beginning teachers more than 20 years ago, before the move toward near constant assessment, there were times when the authors would have welcomed a more systematic approach to figuring out what students knew and did not know. Particularly for beginning teachers, the task of determining what students understand and whether instructional activities are effective, and for whom, can be overwhelming. The move toward making data analysis a part of teaching gives educators access to information about students that they may not have previously considered.

But there is a risk in the relentless focus on "objective" measures of student performance. While charts and graphs and statistical manipulations can, seemingly, provide the same information about every student, that strength is also a potential flaw, in that it ignores the stories that make up the lives and worlds that fully describe the human beings from whom these statistics are derived. In our own experience as teachers, we find that numbers without story often greatly underestimate the knowledge and potential of young children in particular. Consider two children from a class of first graders for whom Stephanie served as the visiting science teacher. On paper, Denise and Marquise were at two ends of the performance spectrum, particularly in literacy, an area in which Denise performed slightly above grade level (and near the top of her class), and in which Marquise was far below grade level. In addition, Marquise's official school data was most notably marked by frequent discipline referrals and in-school suspensions, data completely absent from Denise's.

Throughout the school year, Stephanie struggled with getting the students in this class to settle and focus, something that was not usually a challenge in her teaching. The students desperately wanted to do the science activities she brought with her each week, yet many days, even with their primary teacher and Stephanie in the room, they struggled to settle enough to even distribute materials. She was teaching this class as part of a research project on how young children come to understand the "big idea" of natural selection in science, and so initially her data collection focused on assessing children's conceptual understanding in multiple ways including interviews, work samples, and videotapes of lessons in action. But increasingly, the chaos and constant disruption of the class took over her attempts to gather her planned data. As her journal devolved into rants of desperation, she decided to forgo her planned research and focus instead on trying to understand the stories of the children with whom she was struggling to connect. She focused on four students in particular who represented particular challenges for her. Two of these were Denise and Marquise. Each week, she tried to write a brief narrative about each child, reflecting how they had taken up the day's science activities and what she was learning about their lives outside of the science classroom.

At first, the narratives for both Denise and Marquise tended to be extremely brief. Denise was what many teachers would consider a "dream student." She was quiet, conscientious, obedient, and hard working. But she rarely spoke, and Stephanie, as a person who makes meaning of the world through words, struggled to really pay attention to this nearly silent child. She sometimes could not remember what Denise had done during class, even 30 minutes afterwards as she sat to write.

Marquise posed the opposite problem. About half of the time he was not in class, having already been removed for a disciplinary issue. But when he was present, he took up a huge amount of teacher time and attention, usually directed at getting him calm enough that other children could settle and work. Stephanie struggled to write about him not due to failure to notice, but because she did not want to write down an account of the constant correction, threats, and negative interactions that left her feeling ineffective. She felt she could not capture Marquise's story because her ability to see it was blocked by her constant negative interactions with him.

Through committing to the process of narrative inquiry, Stephanie found that she needed to focus more of her attention on capturing the moment-to-moment activities of these children that she struggled to understand. She began taking more real-time (though sporadic) notes to capture specific words the children used and to note more methodically their interactions with people and with the science materials. As she did this, the layered stories of these children began to emerge, painting a much richer and more generative picture of their strengths, challenges, and ways of being in the classroom. "What does focus look like?" is a narrative excerpt that came from a synthesis of early notes, and Stephanie's realization that her internal definition of "focused" might need to broaden to include even Marquise, whose explosive behavior often eclipsed but did not erase his love of science.

WHAT DOES FOCUS LOOK LIKE?
(FIRST-GRADE SCIENCE)

Stephanie

Character 1: Denise. Tiny little girl who sometimes reminds me of the butterflies we are studying. At recess, in the tiny, paved area that serves as a playground of sorts, she flits from friend to friend, whispering, giggling, connecting. She spins the rope and her lips move, though even there I don't really hear her voice. But back in class, she lands and holds perfectly still. As children buzz around her, she is the picture of calm. Looking at me, waiting, diligently doing whatever I ask. I distribute magnifiers, and she is the one who waits until I say "go" before picking one up, the one who stays in her seat, carefully examining the tiny caterpillar on the petri dish in front of her, making light, tentative drawings to make sure she has the shape just right. I say write down your ideas, and her pencil is moving, carefully formed letters struggling to spell: "The crisaliss is turning difrint colers. It dose not look like a caterplr now." Then I remind them that some of the science words are on the board. She is the one who finds them in her writing, erases, corrects. In circle discussions, she listens, tracks the speaker, nods, smiles. She answers if I ask her to, sometimes even raises her hand of her own accord. And when it is time for me to leave, her eyes track me to the door, her hand waving slightly as a cacophony of classmates' voices shout goodbyes.

Character 2: Marquise. On days he has already been kicked out of class before science time, I can tell when I walk in the room, as the air is either a bit less kinetic or even more charged than normal. After Marquise explodes, sometimes a pressure valve is released, and the class calms a bit. Other times it serves as a catalyst. One big explosion, followed by a series of aftershocks. Next Alonzo, then Carissa, and finally Dante, not so loud but spinning, spinning, unable to settle. One day I follow the class in from recess, and he brings me a notebook, says it is his science book. He holds it out to me, but takes a moment to let go when I reach for it. I open it. Page after page of drawings. Mostly buildings and superheroes and monsters. But he says, "no, this part," and flips halfway through. Five pages filled with drawings of insects. "I was watching for them, like you said. They don't all got six legs though. I counted. This one got eight. Spiders. My brother said it's all spiders that got eight. But I found more ladybugs and they're six." In that moment, I do not know quite what to say. "Wow, Marquise, you've done a lot of observing! What a scientist you are. Will you share this with the class?" He nods, takes the book back. But by the time we have gotten settled in our science circle, his teacher has removed him to settle an earlier playground conflict. When they return, children are setting up their ladybug tests and don't have the patience to look at his notebook. He clutches it in one hand, then puts it under his petri dish, then uses it to block his work from the sight of others. He gets very little done during science time, but the notebook is in contact with some part of his body for the next 30 minutes, until at last we are in the circle again, and he is showing us his eight legged and six legged creatures. He is tentative at first, unused to sharing his scientific work. But as classmates admire his drawings, a broad smile gathers on his face, and even his body becomes a bit more still.

Who is focused? What does the term even mean?

These early attempts at uncovering the narratives of these students' school lives gradually transformed her interactions with Marquise (although he was still removed from class on a regular basis). As her notes and subsequent narratives developed, however, she was disturbed by how hard it was for her to pay attention to Denise, how she had to use color-coded post-it notes to force herself to remember to write specific observations of this quiet, obedient child. She realized she was sometimes frustrated that Denise did not speak up or exercise much social power in the class. Why on earth did she feel frustrated over an angelic six-year-old who hung on her every word? One day while compiling notes, a memory of her own schooling came to her, a story she has told often to both children and university students to explain her own growth as a learner. As she wrote down this piece of her own school story, she saw how her own definition of "good student," once seemingly similar to Denise's, was now in complete conflict with this child's school-perfect behavior (see "Calculus, Voice, and The Fear of Silence"). As the year went on, Stephanie began to have more one-on-one conversations with Denise, who it turned out was eager to share her ideas when asked. Stephanie nudged her a bit to be braver in her scientific drawings, to be willing to have a less than perfect image in her notebook. But she also worked to remind herself that quiet attentiveness can be an incredible asset to a scientist, and she worked to acknowledge not Denise's obedience, but her attention to detail and careful observation.

CALCULUS, VOICE, AND THE FEAR OF SILENCE (FIRST-GRADE SCIENCE)

Stephanie

In 11th grade, I ended up in an advanced calculus class generally meant for seniors, a place I felt I didn't belong from the very first day. I spent the entire year doing all the things I had done to be a "good student" for the past 12 years of my school life. I sat quietly in class, facing forward and taking copious notes. I only raised my hand if I was sure I had the correct answer, which meant in this class my hand rarely left my side. I studied on my own for tests. When I got them back with more red marks than I had ever seen on a paper of mine before, I was dismayed. But I kept enacting the same good student behavior I knew, because it never occurred to me to do anything else. I learned one new skill that year, to ask a friend for help. I spent hours on the phone with Gillian, a math whiz friend with endless patience, and thanks to her I made it through the class. But I reached the end of the year knowing that I truly had not understood a single thing we did all year in that class. And that the following year I would be in a special intermediate calculus class with only six highly motivated, far more skilled classmates who all clearly belonged in this high level class. I lost sleep that summer imagining the shame I would feel, exposed as a fraud among these geniuses. Then something clicked in me and I made a decision. I would rather declare myself unknowledgeable than feel the shame of hiding it. By 10 minutes into class on the first day of senior year, my hand was in the air. "Mr. Goodman, I have no idea what you just explained." And Mr. Goodman, for the first of a thousand times to come, stopped mid-lecture and explained again. Because of my fear of failure mingled with Mr. Goodman's endless good humor, I changed who I was as a student that year, from quiet and obedient to somewhat fearless.

I was a high privilege student when I made that change. I went to a specialized high school, I was receiving the best education my district had to offer, and I was in the top math class in the school. I was also an affluent, white student who the people around me labeled as smart, capable, and likely to go far in school. Am I expecting six-year-old Denise to make the leap that I was only able to make as a 17-year-old, with every possible circumstance working in my favor? And is my new way of being a "good student" really superior to Denise's way? I imagine that in many classrooms, the assertive behavior I hope to see in Denise would not be rewarded as much as her quiet competence.

What Stephanie gained from this turn toward narrative inquiry did not negate what she learned from more traditional data collection methods (although this certainly could have been the case). Denise far outperformed Marquise on measures of content understanding at the end of the year. However, Stephanie did find that her own bias had led to her somewhat ignoring that, based on interview data (as opposed to written assessment), Marquise had the second highest level of understanding of the science concepts at the start of the year. But more importantly, engaging in narrative inquiry, searching for and using stories from multiple vantage points to understand classroom activity, Stephanie was able to question ultimately unhelpful assumptions she made about her students as learners and as people. She was able to consider her students' narratives in relation to her own and in so doing expand her own understanding of what it might mean to be focused and engaged in learning.

If we view teaching as a primarily relational act, then to improve teaching, we must improve our understanding of the relationships developed in classrooms as well as the relationships outside of the classroom that inform the stories of those within. The act of looking for stories changes what we attend to in classrooms. While traditional assessment data necessarily narrows our focus to a specific skill or concept, narrative inquiry forces us to also use a broader lens, to understand such information as part of a larger story of a child's life.

Working to construct narratives also makes us aware of holes in our understanding. Stephanie's initial data collection made clear a literal hole, her lack of attention to Denise and students like her. And then once she began to create narrative accounts of Denise's classroom life, she found another hole, one in her own understanding and empathy for students like Denise. In telling, making meaning of, and revising the stories of her classroom, Stephanie was able to confront her own biases based on her past experiences as a learner and a teacher, and to work to create shared stories with a group of students with whom she struggled mightily. This focus on creating shared meaning is a core way in which narrative inquiry can be used by teachers to examine and many times modify their own practice. When we are attending to the stories of those around us, it is nearly impossible to keep our own story entirely separate from theirs.

Narrative in the Age of Standards

American education is in the midst of an "Age of Standards," in which clearly defined goals and measurable objectives, standardized across districts, states, and much of the nation, are considered the gold standard of a well functioning education system. While the K–12 arena has focused on set academic standards for many years, there is a growing movement to also base early childhood education on age-specific academic standards and goals (NAEYC, 2012). Yet there is nothing even remotely standardized about narrative inquiry. Is this, then, a terrible time to promote narrative inquiry as a means of professional growth?

We propose that the insights available through the methodology of narrative inquiry provide an important counterbalance to the current focus on standards. While it is important to know the expectations and goals for students, and to work toward meeting them, all teachers have encountered the frustration that comes from students not meeting a standard in the way that we hoped. When faced with the feeling of "I taught it! Why didn't they learn it?" we begin to search for alternate approaches and ways to teach more effectively. Sometimes this search for alternatives can feel like a game of chance, picking up a new recommended strategy and hoping that this is the one that will "fix" students' struggles to understand or to master a new skill.

Narrative inquiry takes a step back from our rush to fix things, instead requiring us to understand the intertwined and complex stories that are embodied in the people who inhabit our classrooms. When we are seeking to understand students' and teachers' stories, we are slower to try to fix them. And sometimes this shift, from repairperson to storykeeper, can result in new ways of engaging with the standards as well as with our students.

Narrative and Inquiry for Professional Growth

Research has shown that *teacher reflection and self-study* are promising avenues for professional growth in early childhood (Edwards, Gandini, & Forman, 2012; Kastle, 2012; Kroll & Meier, 2015; Perry, Henderson, & Meier, 2012) and in elementary school and beyond (Cochran-Smith & Lytle, 1993, 1999; Goswami & Stillman, 1987; Lewis, 2009; Loughran & Russell, 2002; Zeichner, 1994). Teachers engaged in this process become more astute observers of students, more perceptive on how to improve their teaching practices, understand the teaching-learning process more deeply, and become more invested in their professional life as an educator who can make a difference for students, families, institutions, and communities. Forms of teacher reflection and self-study are emphasized in a range of preservice teacher education programs, and though to a lesser extent, are featured in inservice professional development goals and programs in schools and districts.

Within the overall framework of reflective practice and self-study, *narrative inquiry* has yet to play a prominent role in either preservice or inservice teacher education and professional growth. This is perplexing given the longstanding human propensity to observe and understand and act on the world via stories passed down through cultures, generations, and geographic location. Teachers spend a good part of their daily lives exchanging stories to share common problems and triumphs, problem-solve sticky situations, seek camaraderie, relieve stress, and generally improve as an individual and educator.

The inclusion and integration of a narrative approach to teaching can inculcate a continually open and fresh approach to the benefits, joys, hardships, and even the mysteries of teaching well. There are four central elements of a well-told story that affect the personal and professional lives of educators, and influence professional growth and development over time—it's genuine and rings true; it invites reflection and discourse; it is interpreted and reinterpreted; and it is powerful and evocative (Jalongo & Isenberg, 1993). Stories of educational practice, and idea-making and theorizing, from the inside of classrooms appeal to practitioners—they "get to the heart of the matter" and help "achieve a multiplicity of perspectives" (Jalongo, 1995, p. 14).

Summary

In this book we approach narrative inquiry for teaching as both a research methodology and an ongoing practice that can become part of teachers' work to document, reflect upon, and improve their practice. The chapters that follow take up specific issues relevant to developing a manageable, ongoing process of narrative inquiry for teaching: identifying puzzles and problems of practice which can be explored through narrative inquiry; developing tools for documentation and collection of narratives from multiple perspectives; considering ways to collect stories of children and in some cases include them as co-inquirers; using narrative inquiry as a tool for curricular reform; and using narrative inquiry specifically to investigate issues of language and literacy. We invite you to explore these chapters in the order that best meets the need of your own emerging practice as narrative inquirer, and to consider how this rich methodology can inform and transform your practice.

2

PROBLEMS AND PUZZLES FOR INQUIRY

What Story Are We Telling?

What is Research? Alina's Dilemma

Somewhere in our schooling, we all learned "the research process," perhaps under its most common name, "the scientific method." Each person reading this likely learned early on, as we did, that research begins with identifying a measurable, "researchable" question, preferably one that actually needs answering. The researcher then uses what is already known about the problem to develop a hypothesis as to what data might show. She designs a methodology to test only the identified variable, and to control all other factors. Often, statistical analyses help specify the degree to which the intended intervention is related to any observed effects. Finally, based on the analysis, the researcher develops conclusions to be shared with, critiqued by, and ideally replicated by others in the field.

In recent years, there has been much debate over whether this methodology does, in fact, represent an idealized research process, or whether it is only one of many ways that scientists and other researchers engage in inquiry. Most educators and researchers agree that "the scientific method," still taught widely in schools from preschool to college, is at best an overly simplistic model that shows only one of the myriad processes used to develop and test hypotheses. Many researchers across fields argue that the preeminence of this particular set of steps in our collective knowledge bases prohibits more expansive notions of what it means to explore important questions and build new, relevant, and transferable knowledge (c.f. Windschitl, Thompson, & Braaten, 2008; Rifkin, 2009).

And yet the texts of our field still pay homage to this methodology at every turn. Elementary school science fairs are a great place to find evidence that "the scientific method" is forced onto us at a very young age, even when it doesn't make sense. Anyone who has read an ill-formed hypothesis about what baking soda and vinegar have to do with volcanoes will see the problem with forcing a methodology onto an exploration that does not really begin or end with a hypothesis.

Likewise, the typical chronology and names of "the scientific method" components undergird author guidelines for most academic journals in education as well as the guidelines for MA and doctoral students completing research theses. However, there is wide agreement that the ideal of the large-scale, controlled test cannot possibly reveal all that is needed to understand the complex social world of schools and classrooms (Berliner, 2002; Rowbottom & Aiston, 2006). Educational researchers have long drawn from many other types of inquiry to seek understanding of children, teachers, and the academic worlds that they inhabit.

One of the things that becomes apparent when conducting research of any type in a classroom is that staying focused on a predetermined research question can pose an extraordinary challenge. Things rarely unfold as anticipated in a classroom, and what is interesting or worth studying often becomes apparent only as the researcher begins to collect some sort of data. This is even more likely to be true if the researcher is also the teacher in the classroom. While focus on a particular issue or question is essential in order to make meaning of the huge amount of input coming at the teacher/researcher every minute, initial forays into systematic recording of data often reveal that the problem most in need of studying is not the problem that is originally identified. This issue may, at first, seem amplified when engaging in narrative inquiry, as early attempts at recording stories of the classroom can look like a pile of unrelated anecdotes. Or the teacher researcher may feel the pull to develop a narrative that matches her question, even if her heart tells her this isn't the story she is really seeing unfold.

Take for example Alina Gish, a masters degree student and first-grade teacher, who set out to study whether a new, schoolwide social emotional curriculum had the intended positive impact on her students. She began with a broad question typical of the type of curriculum efficacy investigations teacher researchers often take up: How effective is this specific social emotional curriculum with the linguistically and culturally diverse students in my classroom? She had outcome data from studies of the curriculum in settings very different than her own, and she set out to collect similar data from her own class, to see if the effects in her urban, low-income school with a student body made primarily of students of color were similar to those in the predominately middle-class schools that had been tested in the pilot. She did not intend for her study to be a narrative inquiry, but she decided to journal about how the intervention was unfolding, and thus ended up with a set of narratives about her practice and about what and whom she attended to during these sessions.

As she collected her data on students' pro-social data, she noticed a few things. First, although it appeared that many students were learning the strategies of the new curriculum, the classroom remained fairly chaotic, and this seemed to be largely because of two particular students whose behavior fell far outside the norm. Second, she found that all of her narrative journal entries centered around these two boys, since so much of her time and energy went to addressing their behavior. Finally, she found that she did not really care much about her study. She cared about finding an intervention that would help her two struggling students, and less about how the intervention tweaked the already mostly pro-social behaviors of her other students. She struggled with the implications of changing her study for several weeks: She had already framed her study, so would it be okay to change the focus? And would following just one or two students really "count" as a study? To Alina, switching her focus from the whole class to only her two most struggling students felt like losing her study.

Overwhelmed by data, she eventually decided to give it a try. At about the time she made this switch, the behavior of one boy had begun to be less disruptive. So she focused on only one child, "Roger." For six months, she recorded stories of Roger in the classroom, both while explicitly teaching the new curriculum and at other points in the school day. She video-recorded lessons and counted the number of pro-social and anti-social behaviors Roger exhibited. As her story became more and more focused on this one child, she unfortunately found herself feeling less and less effective as a teacher. She had reams of data in the form of teacher narratives, observational codes, and written assessments, and she had "shown" with rigor that the curriculum as implemented was not working with Roger. She was disheartened and frustrated as she realized her first study was going to be about what she felt was her complete failure to connect with and assist a struggling child.

Alina spent hours pouring over her data, and she began to see two things that her own growing narrative of failure had obscured. First, she revisited her decision to drop the second student, John, as a subject of her inquiry. She spent some time watching him carefully in the classroom and capturing stories of his interactions with other students and adults. She realized that his classroom story had transformed over the course of the year. On a day-to-day basis, he exhibited virtually none of the problematic behaviors that had defined her interactions with him earlier in the year. By focusing on the one child for whom none of her attempts seemed to work, she had developed a story of herself and the curriculum as ineffective. But in fact, John's story, when re-examined, provided a strong counter-narrative.

Second, she looked back at her interpretation of Roger's orally administered pre- and post-assessments. Roger had actually done extremely well on his post-assessment, indicating that he understood the content of the curriculum and could describe the strategies for positive social behaviors that Alina had spent the year teaching and trying to get her students to practice. Her initial interpretation of this finding was that it did not matter, as his *actual* behavior showed little to no evidence of change in these skills. But as she attempted to recreate John's story and acknowledged that something she had done did seem to have mattered quite a lot for one child, she seemed to develop a potential counter-story about Roger. Perhaps this was not a story of complete pedagogical failure, but a story of not seeing results *yet*. By her openness to continually reexamining and retelling her own narrative, Alina was able to reconsider the stories of both John and Roger in her classroom, and to open up possibilities other than complete success or failure.

But Alina, as with many others new to narrative as a tool of inquiry, struggled with the idea that changing her question and her interpretation in response to unfolding narratives was somehow "cheating" in the research process. She was familiar with and very skilled at using the traditional research paradigm for designing and conducting a study. She knew that the evolving narratives of herself, Roger, and John were critical to understanding what was going on in her classroom, but also that they sometimes did not seem to match her carefully collected quantitative data on specific behaviors. She struggled to see both her "classroom stories" and her coded observational data as valid ways to inform her question. As she went deeper into the data, she began to combine elements of narrative inquiry with her analysis of coded transcripts and student assessment results, allowing her to consider the larger stories of John and Roger that "hard data" alone simultaneously brought to life and obscured. In the end, her masters thesis (Gish, 2015) was a powerful examination of her practice and her relationship with students, and it was significantly different than the study she set out to conduct.

In this chapter, we will explore the often meandering journey of identifying questions and problems for study within the frame of narrative inquiry. Unlike the supposed "scientific method" paradigm, research questions in narrative inquiry do not always precede collection of data, and they often change and develop as stories unfold. While this can feel tremendously uncomfortable for researchers and teachers who have been trained to believe that the pre-designed, controlled test model is the "gold standard" of research, understanding the many ways in which narrative inquiry can unfold may also free us to tell the stories that need to be told, however they emerge in the messy realities of classroom life.

Narrative as a Method to Identify a Persistent Problem

Sometimes narrative inquiries emerge from a set of stories that do not initially seem to have a strong connection. For instance, Stephanie has almost always kept an ongoing teacher journal, and in this she often records stories that show her own unfolding narrative as a teacher in relation with the students she has taught in a wide array of settings, from first grade through doctoral students. Sometimes she collects stories as data for a specific purpose, but often her "teacher stories" are simply a way to reflect on the day or week and to plan next steps.

The habit of collecting and composing narrative about teaching, though, sometimes reveals a persistent problem of practice that Stephanie eventually realizes she has begun puzzling over long before she officially develops a focused study. Rereading her narratives over time shows her what she spent the most time pondering, what bothers her over and over, what is the same and interesting about the many contexts in which she teaches. For instance, an investigation into how to balance valuing student voice with "covering" a mandatory curriculum emerged from examining a set of classroom stories from the full range of her teaching contexts over several years: a first-grade classroom in a low-income community in which she was a "guest science teacher" conducting a study about children's scientific knowledge development; a doctoral course on student development in math and science for an educational leadership program that included school leaders in pre-K through college-level settings; and a fifth-grade class at a small independent school in which she taught environmental science. The excerpts below show parts of narratives she wrote in each of these settings:

FIRST-GRADE SCIENCE, DECEMBER 2010

Today worms changed my life. For the past several weeks, I have felt myself transforming into "bossy mean teacher" as I step into the classroom each week. Outside, as I arrive and see the kids at recess in their tiny, paved outdoor area with no play equipment other than a couple of balls and a huge supply of jump ropes, I am all smiles, chatting easily with the crowd of kids who gather to see what I've brought in and to ask what we'll do today. But as these precious six-year-olds file into the classroom post-recess, not yet wound down from the joy and conflicts of their few minutes outside, I feel my face and whole demeanor changing. I remember the squashed caterpillar from the previous week, the screaming fit that ended our science discourse circle the week before, the dozens of interactions that make me doubt that it is possible to teach science well with children I only get to know for an hour each week, whose lives in school and beyond are still almost a complete mystery to me.

So this week, in an effort to shake myself out of an increasingly negative form of interaction, I decide to radically alter my plans. I ditch the plan to start with a directed drawing of our new earthworms. I decide instead to just give everyone their own, individual earthworm, and ask them what they can figure out. I make two rules: You need to stay at your table, and you must keep your earthworm safe from harm.

Nearly an hour later, with great hesitation, I stop them so we can share out. During the entire science time, there has been not one overly disruptive behavior. Some children have developed complex tests of whether their worm prefers darkness or light, the damp paper towel or the dry paper plate. One child asked for brown paper to put on the plate so she could figure out if it was the brownness or the wetness that made the worm head back for the paper towel every time. Other students do not appear to have "done" much of anything. They have gazed at their worm, held it, let it crawl across their journals. But I decided that for today, I would let them do as they pleased, regardless of what I hoped for. The peaceful, happy hour that ensued makes me wonder how I can ever justify doing otherwise.

DOCTORAL CLASS, OCTOBER 2013

Lana and Emilio huddled together whispering for most of the 15 minutes I had given students to browse the book options for our final project. I wondered what they were doing, but they seemed to want privacy, so I left them alone. At the end of class, they approached me and told me they wanted to propose their own book choice for the project, rather than choosing from my pre-selected volumes. They described the book, *Sensipensante* (Rendon, 2009), noting point after point of how it was related to the themes of the class. I noticed Lana looking down and saw she had written notes to guide her argument as she spoke. I told them that the book sounded perfectly suited to the course, and I asked if either of them had a copy I could borrow so that I could do a quick check for content, since I was completely unfamiliar with the author. Both offered to bring me copies and, to be honest, looked surprised that I agreed so easily. I have had the following sentence on the assignment description for three years: "Please choose one of the books from this list, or propose an alternate, research-based book that takes up important themes from the course." Lana and Emilio are the first students to ever do so.

FIFTH-GRADE SCIENCE, SEPTEMBER 2014

We are beginning a several month study of energy transfer in ecosystems. By the end of it, I am hoping that children are able to use ideas about photosynthesis, energy transfer from producers to consumers, and natural cycles including the carbon and nitrogen cycles to explain what a "balanced ecosystem" looks like. I also want them to consider humans' role in and impact on a variety of ecosystems. These are ambitious goals for fifth grade, so we wasted no time this morning. After a quick dissection of the word "biology," I introduced the word "ecosystem." By which I mean I said it and told them nothing else. Then I asked them to write in their journals about any prior knowledge, word connections, or other ideas they might have about the term. They consulted with colleagues to expand their ideas, and then I told them that instead of giving them a definition, I wanted to do a simulation with them that would connect to the concept of "ecosystem."

So we headed down to the larger space of the school's community room and I explained the guidelines for our food chain simulation. I explained that everyone would either be a hawk, a rabbit, or a grasshopper, and that everyone could choose what they wanted to be. In this simulation, hawks eat rabbits, rabbits eat grasshoppers, and grasshoppers eat plants. With only those instructions, I asked the group to divide into their chosen animals, and the simulation begin. In the first round, eight children chose to be hawks, six chose to be rabbits, and four chose to be grasshoppers.

When we got to the end of the first round, I recorded the still-living organisms of each type at the beginning and end of the round. Not surprisingly, all that was alive at the end were two hawks and a few plants (pom poms on the ground). We had a brief discussion about why this might be, and then I said we would run the simulation again with the goal of having some of each organism still alive at the end. I said I would turn around and count to 10 slowly, and the group should reorganize in a way that would be more likely to result in balance.

Just as I was getting ready to turn back to face them, the argument began. Several children were saying, "You have to move!" and "Come on, that doesn't make any sense!" Three boys were responding, "We can stay here if we want" and "We get to choose what we are, and I choose hawk." When I turned back around, I saw the problem. Three boys who had been hawks in the first simulation were still standing in the hawk area, and two girls who had been grasshoppers in the first round had also moved to that area. There were still six rabbits, so now there were seven grasshoppers. Several children in the grasshopper area were visibly upset. In part, they were exasperated that the three kids appeared to be acting stubborn. But when I asked them to explain, they reported being upset because they knew everything would still die with so many hawks. I asked the three double-stay hawks what they thought, and one said, "This will work. It makes sense. There's enough rabbits for us." The other two agreed but did not add their thinking. Several students standing in the grasshopper corner were talking over me, insisting that the hawks move. I suggested we run the simulation again to see. This time, at the end, one hawk and one grasshopper remained.

I had everyone sit down in a circle to discuss what we could tell from this second run. One of the hawks said, "It would have worked if we could eat the plants." Another student said she thought this was the point, that hawks don't eat plants, or even grasshoppers. A third student said, "I think if people would just be whatever creature we needed it would work better." Others nodded and snuck glares in the direction of the offending hawks. What was intended to be a fun opening activity was quickly bringing up past conflicts and an intense need for children to defend their positions.

I decided not to spend too much time processing all the underlying issues. I asked instead for everyone to think about how many hawks, rabbits, and grasshoppers they thought would create a situation where some of each creature remained alive at the end. I asked them to hold up fingers to show numbers of each organism. I asked people near the median and outliers to explain their reasoning and then took a second survey, and I wrote down numbers based on something close to the median of the second set of responses. I ended up writing two hawks, five rabbits, and 11 grasshoppers on the chart. I assigned roles by just going around the circle, making sure no one who had already been a hawk got to be one again. The simulation went fairly calmly, and at the end they realized they needed to skew the numbers even more toward number of grasshoppers. Then we ran out of time in that class period.

I left the class period wondering if the kids had gotten the point of the simulation at all, or if personal factors and arguing had gotten in the way of science. I had taken a risk, both in leaving the class fully in charge of deciding how many of each organism they should be and in letting each individual choose what role he or she should play. This is a change for me. I have a tendency to be a bit over-controlling in my approach to classroom management, and one of my goals for this year is to be more open to letting things unfold based on students' ideas and responses. But in setting up a difficult situation, letting the children struggle, and then ultimately jumping in to direct the process, I wasn't sure I'd accomplished either scientific or social goals in a meaningful way.

As is often the case, my teacher's view of an incident did not entirely match the students' view. By the time I returned the next week, no one seemed to really remember the conflict, and there was general consensus that we had figured out that there need to be many, many more organisms at the base of a food chain than at the top. But I was reminded how hard it is to enact a commitment to student agency and voice while attending to curricular goals and an ever ticking clock.

Only in the final narrative shown above, after years of collecting "stories of practice" from many teaching settings, did Stephanie pull together a theme that she encountered over and over again throughout the years. Whether in first grade or a doctoral program, she felt both the necessity and the constraints of the core content she was responsible for making accessible to her students. She knew herself to be a highly controlled teacher, approaching nearly every teaching session with a detailed, written plan. On the other hand, she was drawn to interest-driven learning, and she herself hated classroom settings where the teacher acted as the primary purveyor of knowledge. And so she found herself in a constant struggle to balance supporting students' agency and direction of their own learning and a drive to expose students to the many ideas and content areas that they may not yet know enough about to be interested in.

During the four-year period from which the above narratives come, Stephanie's formal research agenda was examining children's cognitive development in relation to a science curriculum that foregrounded the practices of science. She cared deeply about this study, and she steadily collected primarily non-narrative data on children's engagement with and learning of science. But the stories she also collected during this time, almost incidentally at first, and in a more focused way as the project went on, revealed a more personal pedagogical issue that was hidden from her at the outset of the project but that, once revealed, became the issue she knew she *had* to explore in more depth. In the midst of analyzing data for other purposes, she continued to return to the puzzle of how to balance students' interests and voices with the need to follow a well-defined conceptual agenda. And it is the ideas that tell us we *must* take them on that ultimately become sustainable topics for classroom-based inquiry.

Taking four years (or 20) to identify a research problem may seem a bit extreme. But narrative often works this way. The stories of the lives and relationships that teachers develop in their classrooms unfold over days and weeks, but also over years and decades. The turning of our attention to different aspect of these shared spaces is inevitable as our practice changes, matures, and sometimes breaks down or undergoes transformation; as each year's students enter, grow, and leave; as the curricular and policy landscape around us changes, sometimes causing earthshaking changes, other times bringing into clarity what we most value and what we do not.

Having a research question is an important aspect of moving from the collecting of stories and reflections toward narrative as research methodology that can affect one's teaching practices. But the question that we start with is very often not the question that emerges as most important if we listen to what the collected stories are telling us.

Multiple Narratives to Confront the Danger of a Single Story

> Stories matter. Many stories matter. Stories have been used to dispossess and to malign, but stories can also be used to empower and to humanize. Stories can break the dignity of a people, but stories can also repair that broken dignity. (Adichie, 2009)

Teachers hold incredible power, despite our frequent realizations that there are areas in which we are also utterly powerless. Most educators have had experiences that bring to life both extremes. In our own classrooms, we have the power to shape the stories of our students, who have less power because of their age, their status as students, the culture of schooling that places teachers in positions of authority, and often because of differences of class and race between the teacher and his pupils. In relation to our students, there is generally a power differential that results in the educator coming out on top.

In the larger world of educational policy and societal views at large, though, American teachers rarely feel such power. Although we the authors are currently primarily university faculty, we both came from and maintain connection to the world of children's schooling, and so we can only describe this powerlessness by identifying with pre-K and elementary teachers as "we." We are blamed for brokenness in the system that could not possibly be caused by individual teachers. We often stand by helpless as even people personally close to us seem to absorb the stories told by societal power-holders more readily than the very personal counter-narratives we offer in the form of our lives and relationships. Any teacher who has ever been told that he is "one of the good ones" has felt the powerlessness that comes from this attribution. In other words, our story has not changed the speakers' core belief about teachers' lack of intelligence/easy work hours/fat pensions. We have been written off as an exception to a deeply believed "truth."

In the same manner, students may feel powerless to change the dominant narrative about who they are, how they learn, and what they deserve. When the teacher is the sole teller of the story of the class, despite the large cast of characters, the students lose the power of owning their own narrative, and thus having the ability to examine, own, and perhaps even change it. Chimamanda Ngozi Adichie recounts:

> Power is the ability not just to tell the story of another person, but to make it the definitive story of that person. The Palestinian poet Mourid Barghouti writes that if you want to dispossess a people, the simplest way to do it is to tell their story and to start with, "secondly." Start the story with the arrows of the Native Americans, and not with the arrival of the British, and you have an entirely different story. Start the story with the failure of the African state, and not with the colonial creation of the African state, and you have an entirely different story. (Adichie, 2009)

When a teacher starts the story of a student, he most likely starts, unwittingly, with the "secondly." That is, he has access to the story that begins as the child enters his classroom. What is missing is the story of the child's family, her relationship with siblings, her grandparents' experiences that help shape the glimpse of a story that a teacher sees in just a few hours a day, for just a few months of a lifetime.

When we invite children to construct narratives as part of our research, the questions we may have started out asking begin to change and develop in response to these new and often shockingly different vantage points. Several years ago, a fifth-grade teacher, Tiffany, came into Stephanie's MA class on conducting teacher research and sighed as she dropped a pile of papers on the table. When the group checked in, Tiffany was clearly distressed. She said she had decided to add student reflections to her data on using multiple math problem solving strategies with fifth graders. She had students write for a few minutes at the end of each class period using a very open ended prompt suggested by a colleague in the class: What went well? What would you change? The students eagerly wrote, and she collected two weeks of reflections from all of them, but she had not really looked at them until the hours leading up to the class session. When she did, she was disheartened. Instead of writing about the problem solving strategies she was studying and working so hard to teach, almost every child had written about social dynamics in their groups. Some talked about certain children "taking over" the problem-solving sessions, telling everyone else what to put on their papers. Others said their partners worked too slowly, and it was frustrating to wait for them to catch up. One child wrote that what had gone well one day was that the class wasn't very long.

Tiffany passed samples around to prove the uselessness of the reflections for her inquiry into which problem solving strategies were most effective. She said she had wasted a lot of instructional time for nothing. Not surprisingly, the rest of the teachers in this MA class more quickly saw what she was not yet seeing: Her students were telling her a different, and perhaps more important, story. The social interactions in their problem solving groups were taking precedence over mathematical strategies, as emotional issues often do. The student reflections were giving her valuable information about questions she needed to be asking about how her students were experiencing math class. Her own story, as someone who only recently but passionately embraced exploring multiple methods of problem solving, was covering up an alternate narrative of children who were not yet in a comfortable space to engage in the practices she was excited to teach them.

It was frustrating and uncomfortable for this teacher to temporarily let go of her well-formed, interest-based research question and take up a question based on the narratives of her students: How do we create the social structures needed to engage in complex problem solving? But in doing so, she invited her students to tell their stories and granted them power and voice in both the classroom and the research process.

For younger children, inviting children to tell their own stories rarely involves long, written narratives. It may instead look like an ongoing conversation between teacher and child, or the teacher attending carefully to conversations between children, withholding interpretation and instead looking for the questions that matter most to the children. Consider, for instance, the interactions described below, between three preschool teachers and their students after the discovery of a snail.

A DISCOVERY ON THE SIDEWALK

At a meeting of Las Americas Early Education Center Inquiry Group, which Daniel co-facilitates with one of the head teachers, Michael Escamilla, in San Francisco, Michael told the group of his initial discovery of a snail on the sidewalk and Saraha and Alicia, his co-teachers, add to the unfolding snail project . . .

Michael: I saw a snail on the sidewalk one morning a few weeks ago as I walked to school. I picked it up with a napkin and took it to school. I had no idea that this snail would spark the children's interest and turn into a project that brought in language, art, and science.

Saraha: The children talked about the snail that morning in Spanish and I wrote down what they said. (Saraha turns the pages of her documentation book, consisting of her photographs and the children's dictation and drawings of the snail.) This is [Child 1]'s dictation in Spanish that the snail was sticky. I had brought in some books from the library and [Child 2] remembered about a wolf snail, which is a carnivore and she remembered that it has what looks like a mustache on it! [Child 3] dictated that the snail has a long neck, and eats small snails and plants. They can put their eyes inside their shells. [Child 3] drew a beautiful drawing of the snail and copied the word "snail" in beautiful writing. [Child 4] dictated that the snail has two small eyes and [Child 5] dictated that the wolf snail has a different shape shell and he drew the snail from a different perspective, angle. We now have two different snails, as I found another one outside. [Child 6] tried to copy the title of the snail book.

Alicia: Here is a published poem about a snail that we included in the book. (Alicia then showed us a published poem about a snail that they included in the documentation book.) The children also did races with the snails on paper and they documented the patterns of the slime trails, and the children dictated their observations of the snail patterns and their movements. We then introduced 10 different line forms, which we printed out and placed in the documentation book. The children were asked if they could predict how the snails might move.

Michael: We had these photos and drawings on the wall last week, and then we took them down and put them into a documentation book format and now we can add more pages. It is portable now and we can take it where we want.

In this case, the teachers did not come into the situation planning to engage in an inquiry at all, other than to simply show the children an interesting creature.

By listening to the children and honoring their stories and interests by recording them, helping them find resources, and creating a documentation book that children could look at over and over, they demonstrated sharing power among teachers and children. They let the children create an inquiry based on their somewhat unexpected (to the teachers) interest, and the teachers took on the role of documenters. Teachers used the child-developed inquiry as a means to investigate some topics in the planned curriculum, as when Alicia described the different line forms and asked the children to make predictions. But the questions, ideas, and stories were based on the children's unfolding narrative, in relation with the adult teachers and, in this case, with the snails.

In both cases above, it is also important to note that more than one adult participated in sharing or co-creating the narratives. In the case of the MA student, her in-class colleagues, unburdened by attachment to her original line of inquiry, were able to gently push her to see the value of her students' counter-narratives. At Las Americas, the entire teaching staff has committed to the practice of documenting children's emerging stories, and they meet regularly to share and examine these narratives. These structures and practices counterbalance the tendency to act as a lone agent in conceptualizing an inquiry, collecting data, and making meaning of it. Explicitly inviting others into one's inquiry, while sometimes uncomfortable, is a necessary step to ensure that research is not based on a single, incomplete story.

Developing questions to guide inquiry is challenging enough when we do it based on our personal, collected stories that reveal what we worry about, what we care about enough to study, what we hope to better understand or to change. Inviting the other members of the classroom community to also tell their stories opens up an element of uncertainty that can be difficult to bear for those of us who are more used to a "clean" research design. But almost without exception, when we and the teachers we have worked with integrate children's and colleagues' stories into emerging inquiries, it becomes clear that our first, teacher/researcher developed questions were one-sided. Challenging ourselves to hear the questions in others' stories, and being willing to change course when a more relevant inquiry reveals itself through these multiple perspectives, shifts the balance of power between teacher/research and child, and has the potential to create an entire classroom full of researchers telling and retelling their narratives, and learning to value the counter-narratives that doubtless exist all around them.

Stories Are Never "Finished"

When teachers begin the process of narrative inquiry in their classrooms, they often run into the problem of the never-ending story. Many teachers turn to narrative inquiry as part of a graduate school program, and such programs require participants to submit a "completed" research study in order to receive the degree. Even those who come to narrative inquiry in ways that do not require such a high-stakes finished product often find themselves frustrated at the lack of endpoints for their work. A teacher who begins to collect stories of her own practice and stories of her students' lives in the classroom, no matter how focused in scope, quickly realizes that there is always more to the story than she has captured at any point in time. As Huber and colleagues note, "Each story, whether personal, social, institutional, cultural, familial, or linguistic, is alive, unfinished, and always in the making; stories continue to be composed with and without our presence." (Huber, Caine, Huber, & Steeves, 2013, p. 16)

How, then, can a teacher researcher make a claim that a study is "complete," when even the questions guiding the inquiry may be in seemingly continuous flux? Addressing this issue requires us to continue the paradigm shift away from the clean, clear lines embodied in the controlled research model we learned earlier in our schooling. The stories of lives in progress are nothing like the reaction of two chemicals to one another, or to the behavior of a new drug to the human body system. When chemicals react, the reaction has a start and an endpoint, and quantifying the reaction can create a full picture of the result. But students' and teachers' lives do not begin and end at the classroom door, and no recording method can fully capture even all of the inter- and intrapersonal relationships that unfold for a single participant over the course of a school day, much less over the course of a year or a childhood or a career.

The stories we collect and examine will always be incomplete. What we choose to examine within these stories will also be only a small portion of "the truth," informed by our current lens of interest, worry, and intent. Tiffany, the fifth-grade teacher studying problem solving, did not at first see the value of her students' narratives, since their focus differed too much from her own. Stephanie pursued a predetermined line of research for several years, knowing that there was another, equally compelling theme to examine in her own teaching narratives. The Las Americas teachers choose a loose area of focus each year to help them in making meaning of their students' emerging stories, but in so doing they are making a conscious choice to focus on one small part of a larger story. And sometimes the chosen focus is pushed aside when a more pressing or cogent theme emerges.

Rather than seeking completeness in our inquiries, perhaps it makes more sense to think of the products we present to the outside world as necessarily small glimpses into the stories and experiences that shape children and teachers. As we develop a habit of examining stories, revising our questions as new parts of the story emerge, and sharing our incomplete but often powerful inquiries with others, we build capacity for truly experiencing the uncertainty and the beauty of human stories lived out in and beyond our classrooms.

3

NARRATIVE-BASED TOOLS AND STRATEGIES

Telling a Good Story

In this chapter, we discuss several narrative-based tools and strategies that emphasize the linking of text and visuals, journals and diaries, documentation panels and books, and videos and blogs. The tools and strategies come into play once questions and problems have been identified as discussed in Chapter 2. Issues of which narrative-based tools and strategies to use, and when and how, arise early on in a project and one's teaching, and our understanding and intuition for the effective selection of narrative tools eventually becomes "second nature" over time and with practice. At first, the process is a lot of like trying on different shoes, looking for just the right fit and look for one's purposes. So it is natural and beneficial to experiment with a range of narrative-based tools and strategies when starting to maximize the possibilities for observation, documentation, and reflection. This is the casting of a wide narrative net. In keeping with the overall value of narrative inquiry for student learning and teacher growth and reflection as we discussed in Chapter 1, it's also helpful to share stories with colleagues and mentors regarding narrative tools and strategies that we consider both valuable and problematic. The examples that we provide in this chapter are drawn from Daniel's work with the preschool teachers in the Las Americas Inquiry Group, as well as other early childhood and elementary school teachers in the San Francisco Bay area and nationally.

Linking the Personal with the Professional

Well-told inquiry moments and stories often rely on personal and professional connections—a moment, event, or memory from our childhood and schooling become linked with the here and now of our teaching. The effect of this process is a deepening of our emotional response to recasting teaching and learning events and experiences, and a tightening of our personal links to our work with children.

In the example below, Kathie Behlen (2015), a preschool teacher in San Francisco, recounts an outdoor play and discovery scene with her children. Kathie uses the narrative technique of a personal "action-in-memory" via writing to integrate her children's playful exploration with mud and also to link back to her own personal memories of playing with mud as a young child. The effect of this action-in-memory is a storied reflection that reinforces and validates Kathie's teaching philosophy of children's playful exploration of the physical properties of nature and science.

MAKING A MUD KITCHEN
(Behlen, 2015)

The first thing I wanted to implement was creating a mud kitchen for the toddlers and twos. The toddlers in my classroom had shown great interest in "domestic" dramatic play and I had brought old pots and pans from my house to experiment with in the sandbox (Figures 3.1 and 3.2).

I had the children help me gather "ingredients" around the yard and on our walks to cook with including herbs, leaves, flowers, weeds, and pinecones.

FIGURE 3.1 Playing with pots. [Photo credit: Kathie Behlen]

FIGURE 3.2 Gathering ingredients. [Photo credit: Kathie Behlen]

This was a new experience for both the children and me because before the children did not have access to natural materials other than sand and wood blocks. After a couple of weeks of the children still being interested in this play, I began to make plans on how to construct a real mud kitchen. I decided to put it in a corner near the back of the yard because this space was underutilized, it had a water source nearby, and it was a separate area where the children could get messy without disturbing the infants. When discussing these plans with my co-teachers I realized that this messy, sensory area was really important to me and is an experience that I had as a child (Figure 3.3).

FIGURE 3.3 Kathie as a child playing in the mud. [Photo credit: Kathie Behlen]

I had a personal interest in this project since it brought up many childhood memories about messy mud play days in my backyard (as shown in the picture above), digging tunnels, and worm hunting. I feel since I have such positive, strong memories about getting messy as a child, these values impact the things I want to do with the children and what I find acceptable for the children to do. Other teachers who may have grown up in an urban area with less access to natural, messy play may not feel this aspect of our outdoor space is as important as I do. However, despite conflicting views on how messy the children should get, all of the teachers were on board with the construction of a mud kitchen. Our final "budget" mud kitchen was completed when I sealed and glued cinder blocks together and added two panels of wood on top for a make shift countertop space. I loved the look of the natural wood and the little cubbies in the cinder blocks that children could hide and store their treasures in. Next we added a plastic picnic table and kitchen with an oven that was donated from a family that no longer wanted them. Although it does not look like it is worth a million dollars, it suits our purpose for muddy, natural play!

Turning Text and Visuals into Narratives

Like a powerful painting, visuals are central to telling a memorable story. In creating a narrative about a project or series of activities or lessons, there are certain characteristics of visuals that inform the narrative product:

- A single image can tell a whole story.
- A series of images can tell the constituent parts of a story.
- Visuals speak also to our sense of aesthetics.
- Visuals can save text and words.
- Visuals can tell part of a story that words can't or don't tell well.
- Visuals can convey a sense of space, dimension, color, tone.
- Visuals can lend themselves to symbolism, simile, metaphor.

When visuals and images are integrated with text, the combination is like an engaging picture book; text and visual work together to illuminate the following narrative elements:

- Character, plot, setting, voice, narration
- Story structure (the unfolding of key events over narrative time and "real" time; an unfolding story arc)
- Evocative power of text and illustration (the story in the text, the story in the pictures, their "combined" story)
- Aesthetics and artistry of word choice (the power of the language of stories)

This integration happens on a few critical narrative levels. First, the text tells the "main" story and provides the narration that drives the telling. Second, the images can depict the story of the text, and images can also tell a story or part of a story not told or referred to in the text. Third, when text and visuals work together they combine to create a third narrative level. All three levels inform the listener, reader, and observer of a well-told story with multiple levels, representations, and meanings.

Children's picture books provide extraordinary examples of well-told stories that integrate text and visuals.

A brief look at a few children's picture books reveals how this medium achieves the artistry of text and visual integration that creates well-told, engaging stories that allow us to see phenomena more deeply socially, culturally, and psychologically. In Nina Crews's (2006) *Below*, Crews uses text and photography to tell the story of a young boy's lost toy, and how he enlists his other toys to search for and finally recover the lost toy. In Grace Lin's (1999) *Ugly Vegetables*, Lin uses watercolors and poignant language to tell the story of conflict and then understanding between a Chinese-American mother and her daughter. In Alma Flor Ada's (2004) *With Love, the Little Red Hen* (illustrated by Lesley Tryon), Ada uses the genre of letters to create a playful retelling of well-known story replete with a cast of literary characters.

Let's now look at two narrative inquiry examples of integrating text and visuals that tell two different stories of professional insight and growth.

Cultural and Community Empowerment—Renetta Goeson

Renetta Goeson, who currently works as a training specialist for Head Start programs in South Dakota, tells the story of her prior work as a director of a tribal Head Start program in South Dakota. Renetta's narrative inquiry product is a published article (Goeson, 2014) in a journal devoted to early childhood teacher research. Her story is intended for other early childhood educators, researchers, and others interested in promoting inquiry and reflection in early childhood.

Renetta uses the framework of narrative inquiry to understand and tell the story of her work on her reservation, Lake Traverse. Using a mix of written stories and anecdotes, poetry, historical artifacts, and photographs, Renetta recounts key elements and beliefs from her Dakota background and history to illuminate essential aspects of her work with children, teachers, and families. Her text is based on Renetta's notes, journal entries, interviews with elders and family members, personal reflections, and oral stories. For example, Renetta used an excerpt from her interview with her grandmother, in which her grandmother tells the story of the injustices she endured as a young child.

Honoring the traditional reverence for elders and ancestors, Renetta recounts her identity through the history of her name. She does this by writing about the origins of her name—to understand who she is, Renetta must understand and

AN INTERVIEW WITH MY GRANDMOTHER—AMELIA (OWEN) GERMAN
(Goeson, 2014)

(reprinted with the author's permission)

When I was six years old, I was forced to go away to a boarding school in Pipestone, Minnesota. They came to the reservations and took all the Native American children and put us on a train and sent us off to school. This school was no good, it was like a prison. We had to get up early and march in a line to breakfast. After breakfast we had to do the dishes then we went to school all day. We could only speak English, if we were caught speaking our Native language we were punished. Many of the students could not speak English very well, because they only spoke their Native language at home, so this was very difficult for them. At night we had to clean our dormitories, we worked very hard and were watched closely. We were all very tired most of the time and very homesick. We were treated very badly. I only went to school there for a year, but it seemed like a very long time.

remember where she came from and how her name both symbolizes and connects her to her ancestors and to the place of her ancestors. Within this powerful tradition of storytelling, stories help link Renetta back to her roots and to sacred touchstone traditions and values, and it is this process of going back (or storying back) that allows Renetta to reaffirm who she is at the present and to go forward in her work.

WOYAKE MITAWA (MY STORY)
(Goeson, 2014)

My own story begins with my name. Who am I? My Dakota name is Pte Duta Win (Red Buffalo Woman); this name was given to me by a Wakan Wicasta (Medicine Man) later in life. Typically a person receives their Dakota name as a child, however, for unknown reasons my parents did not give me one while I was young. To the Dakota people, one's name is very important. It is commonplace to have both an English and a Dakota name. My English name, Renetta, was derived from blending the names of two tribal elders, Rena DeCoteau and Etta Thompson, as they both requested that my mother name me after them. It is an honor to be named after such respected and strong Dakota women, who have made a positive impact on the community. Rena was a caring mother and grandmother, and Etta was part of the first Human Service Board on the Lake Traverse Reservation. Her commitment to the health of the community has left a legacy. I am very proud to be their namesakes. Growing up among the trees, I have a deep respect for them not only because they are deeply rooted in Mother Earth, but also because I symbolically view a tree's roots as my ancestors, the beginning of our story of who we are as family. I am but one branch of this tree.

For visuals, Renetta includes such varied elements as her own original painting and drawing depicting her ancestral tree and a mother and child, a map of the Great Sioux Nation, photographs from museums and historical societies of elders and Native American children involuntarily attending boarding schools, photographs of her family members, and a calendar depicting Dakota beliefs around the seasons and animal life (Figures 3.4, 3.5, and 3.6).

Renetta's story, told via text and visuals, is an aesthetic integration of oral and written language that honors the storytelling traditions of the Dakota, and shows how educators can use narrative inquiry "to recover their voices and reclaim their knowledge and understanding of what they do as central and legitimate sources of information about teaching young children" (Stremmel, 2014, p. 1). Renetta combines visuals and text to tell a personal and professional early childhood story that is rooted in her people's history of dehumanization and disenfranchisement in and out of educational settings. Her narrative account, as told

FIGURE 3.4 Renetta's paternal grandmother, Bessie Ironheart. [Photo credit: Renetta Goeson]

FIGURE 3.5 Mother and child. [Artwork credit: Renetta Goeson]

FIGURE 3.6 Ancestral roots. [Artwork credit: Renetta Goeson]

in her selected images and words, shows us how deeply such injustices can and will leave their "mark" on families and in one's "psyche" (p. 11), affecting the core of Renetta's educational beliefs, vision, and work with children, teachers, and families.

Documenting the Story of a Collage Project—Michael Escamilla

Michael Escamilla and his colleagues (Alicia Alvarez, Sahara Gonzalez, Mary Lin, Edwin Serrano, and Joanne Yu) teach in a dual language preschool (one classroom uses Spanish and English, the other classroom uses Cantonese and English) that also features a project-based curriculum (Katz, Chard, & Kogan, 2014), where projects are based on children's interests and can last for several weeks or months. Michael and his colleagues also emphasize an arts-based curriculum fashioned after the Reggio Emilia schools of Northern Italy (Edwards, Gandini, & Forman, 2012), as well as an adaptation of Reggio's (Rinaldi, 2001) use of documentation to represent text and visuals via books, panels, videos, and photographs that tell a story of particular project or set of learning experiences.

Michael (2013) took photographs and wrote down observational notes to document the children's engagement during the collage project, and this material served as an in-process form of reflection for Michael and his colleagues to make changes both in their teaching and in their documentation. Then when the collage project reached its natural conclusion after five months, Michael selected those photographs that he thought told the most effective story of the children's interests in and creation of collages, and then wrote up his observational notes into extended prose to describe and reflect on the benefits of the collage project and how it might be improved. Put together, the in-project and end-of-project documentation allows Michael to reflect on learning patterns and learning connections that he and his colleagues might have missed while teaching. Initially, as is typical of Michael's documentation, he was not looking to tell any particular teaching or learning story with the collages.

Not forcing the evolution of the project, and not sure where the collage engagement would lead, Michael "wanted to record the children's imaginative process and find the value of rich open-ended activities where the children could work at their own pace, liberate themselves from the constraints of ditto sheets or outlines, and tap into their creative selves" (p. 4). Michael's selection of key anecdotes from his written notes and the most telling photographs from his collection also allowed Michael to create mini-profiles and portraits of individual children's collage work as well as the collages that Michael, Joanne, and Sahara each created, too. This is a small version of portraiture (Lightfoot, 1983; Lawrence-Lightfoot & Hoffmann Davis, 1997), an approach to storytelling and research that provides a picture or portrait of a student, teacher, project, classroom, program, or school with an eye toward creating an aesthetically pleasing product. In this case, Michael's written and visual story tells the process and products of a shared project in which the children and the teachers all created collages.

For example, looking back on the five months of the collage project, Michael knew that the children had worked individually, in pairs, and in small groups painting and repainting their canvases and selecting materials to add. In reviewing his notes and photographs, Michael noticed that one small design innovation in one child's collage sometimes led to changes in another child's collage. He noticed that "Edgar placed several triangles on the edge of his large, rectangular collage (Figure 3.7) giving the impression of a frame, Maria liked his idea and she also used triangles to place around her canvas, but she also added paper rollups and dried flowers in between the triangles (Figure 3.8) on both sides to create her own design" (p. 3).

Michael's selection of key anecdotes from his written notes and the most telling photographs from this collection also allowed Michael to look closely at his teaching role. For instance, Michael examined his interactions with Dante and his direct support of Dante's "ladder" collage.

Michael's placing together of his written reflection and the two photographs allows Michael to re-see an important teaching lesson, that direct teacher

FIGURE 3.7 Edgar working on his collage. [Photo credit: Michael Escamilla]

FIGURE 3.8 Maria adding paper rollups and dried flowers to her collage. [Photo credit: Michael Escamilla]

support can help children's creative processes and products, and to highlight a critical moment in the story of Dante's collage—the inclusion of his handprint was a crowning moment for Dante, and the apex of the story arc of his collage process.

DANTE'S COLLAGE
(Escamilla, 2013)

Dante wanted to add his blue handprint on an orange circle under the paper ladder he had constructed and glued on his canvas a few days before (Figure 3.9). Since Dante faced a technical difficulty carrying out his idea, I offered my support by holding the long cardboard canvas in a steady grip while he carefully placed and glued the circle with his handprint in the specific spot where he wanted it. Sometimes children have great ideas but they need adult support to carry them out. From my point of view, adult support to assist a child to make visible his or her idea does not diminish in any way authorship of their work. I have often noticed that teachers, in their efforts not to overtake the child's work, tend to stay away from the creative process and hesitate to offer support, erroneously thinking that if they do then the work produced by the children is not really theirs or authentic enough.

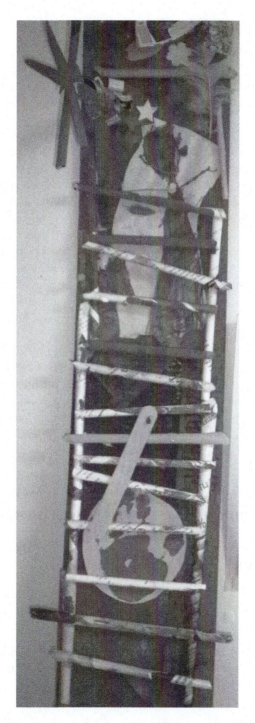

FIGURE 3.9 Dante's handprint under the ladder. [Photo credit: Michael Escamilla]

Observational Notes

The fields of anthropology (Emerson, Fretz, & Shaw, 2011), nature writing (MacDonald, 2015; Zwinger, 1998), and first-person accounts and stories of teaching and learning (Paley, 1981) have long made use of observational notes or jottings for description and analysis. Essentially, these notes add up to small stories about the phenomena or processes observed, and also give insights into the participant/observer's thoughts and feelings. Depending on the field of inquiry and investigation, the goals may change, though in general observational notes are designed to capture and hold one's observations for later analysis and reflection. As such, they are effective narrative tools for capturing and recreating essential elements of a teaching and learning story in and outside of educational contexts.

In the observational notes presented here, Daniel documented his whole-group reading of children's literature and his small-group work with children as they drew and dictated in their personal journals. Daniel wanted his observational notes to document and tell the small moments of the children's language and literacy connections and insights, and also the evolution and story of changes that Daniel made over the course of the year to improve his instruction and the children's learning.

Four months later, as seen in above observational note examples, Daniel had changed his initial notes on the whole-class read-aloud to include his observations on what Daniel called "our old books" (books that Daniel reread for two to three weeks in a row) and "our new books" (unfamiliar books that Daniel introduced at each read-aloud session) with the children. Daniel also streamlined his observational notes to record each child's drawing, dictation, and writing in their personal journals, and to note elements of their work that were the continuation of

---

OBSERVATIONAL NOTES FROM DANIEL'S PRESCHOOL TEACHING

Observational Notes for 10-16-2015, Visit #1

CONTEXT

I read *The Storm Whale* by Benji Davies to the whole class. One boy commented that it was "not safe" for Noi to be home alone. (The text read: "He wouldn't be home again until dark.")

WHAT HAPPENED

As I read, I asked questions:

- about what Noi saw in the distance on the sand (one child said "beach" as I paused) (Text: "It was a little whale washed up on the ____.")
- if whales needed to be in water (they agreed)
- if it was a good idea for Noi to put the whale into the bathtub (a few said it needed water), a few commented that his dad would be mad (Text: "Noi was worried that his dad would be angry about having a whale in the bath")
- I pointed to the lone flipper in the water on the wordless page and pointed out Noi and his dad in their rain jackets, and that "dot dot dot" means something is coming when you see this in a book (Text: "Noi often thought about the storm whale. He hoped that one day, soon . . . "), and asked the class what they saw in the ocean, who might be with the storm whale (can see two fins in the air coming out of the water).

Overall, more boys commented during the read-aloud than girls.

REFLECTIONS

The text in the brackets below denotes potential language to label and categorize problem-solving strategies and elements for the children and myself.

Problem-Solving Strategies and Elements

I. Teacher-Initiated (Daniel)

1. Per textual language ("beach" for "sand") [vocabulary substitution, semantic sets]
2. Per visuals (who was with the whale at the end) [inference from visuals]
3. Per visuals and text as combined (What did Noi see at the end of the beach?) [visual as prompt to interpret text, action, plot]

II. Child-Initiated

1. Child's comment in class that Noi was not safe home alone (social relations, configuration, linking home to school/literacy)

III. Text-Initiated/Structured

1. Provocation and problem at the outset (whale on the sand)
2. Added layer (dad not home)
3. Added layer (Noi alone to problem-solve)
4. Use of tools to problem-solve logistics (cart, bathtub, water, fish)
5. Use of tools to problem-solve social relations ("Somehow Noi kept his secret all evening. He even managed to sneak some supper for his whale.")

ADDITIONAL

I also read with two boys after the whole-group read-aloud. We read all four books that I brought, *The Storm Whale* and *Snail Trail* by Ruth Brown, *Shhh! Don't Tell Mr. Wolf* by Colin McNaughton, and *Gracias/Thanks* by Pat Mora. I asked questions primarily about the visuals to keep them engaged—can you find ___? Where is ___? For instance, we looked for the six cats in *The Storm Whale*, and the boys eagerly counted all six cats on one double-spread page. One student also eagerly counted all 61 bees in one picture of *Gracias/ Thanks*. [Numeracy as linked with literacy, little distinction between the two, as dual symbol systems?]

OBSERVATIONAL NOTES FOR 12-17-2015 VISIT #8

1. Whole Group Read-Aloud

We started by rereading Eric Carle's *Opposites* and *The Bear and Hare*, and read the new book, American Museum of Natural History's *ABC Universe*. They are recalling most of the two familiar books, and enjoyed the new ABC space book. It appears to take three to five times of rereading for a book to take hold, in terms of the children's interest, anticipation of content and form, and the skill in recognizing and contributing to reading engagement in a group.

I also showed the whole class each one of the five children's journal entries who have worked with me; I read the dictation and said one thing about how each child draws, and then we clapped for each child.

2. Individual Journals—Drawing and Dictation

Carlos—Journal #3. He wrote his name on the front and human figure. He then wanted to write Ramirez, and I wrote it in small letters and he copied it in marker next to Carlos. He drew an intricate drawing, in his usual careful and methodological style, all in thin black marker.

He dictated, "This is a big tower" and then he stopped, not wanting to dictate any more. I then asked about the rooms in the tower and whether it was a tall tower. He dictated as he pointed, "Black works on white, and white works on black." He then added, "It has lots of little rooms and one big one for a dinosaur. It's for a T-Rex."

Greg—Drew a number of small marks in his usual style, and then did not want to dictate. I suggested we look at the *ABC Universe* book for an idea. I selected the Comet page since I thought it resembled his drawing. I read the page, hoping Greg would dictate from the text; he said, "Just like that" and pointed to the page. So I wrote down "A comet is a ball of ice and dust," a sentence from the book.

Jason—Drew in green, blue, and purple a swatch in the middle of the page. Did not want to dictate as he wanted to play the bingo game. I said he could dictate later.

Kai—Drew carefully with thin markers for 45 minutes, as is his usual style, and drew two planes, a bus, and a building. He dictated, even stopping a few times so I could catch up, "I took the monorail to our cabin celebration house. We take (then changed it to "took") the bus, took the airplane, and we took another airplane and got there."

Dalisa—Carefully drew a sun and house carefully (as she did last week), but then didn't like it because she put in some red marks in the sun. She then drew on a separate small piece of paper, house and sun and trees, and dictated easily, "I like all of my house and this is for all of my family."

REFLECTIONS

Rereading of read-alouds

Time needed for absorption at individual and group levels—content, form, illustration/photographs, and teacher style of reading (pausing, question, gestures, etc.).

Drawings

Interpretation of one's sense of style vis-à-vis color and form. For example, Carlos's observation today that "black works on white, white works on black."

a pattern (for instance, drawing particular figures or using certain colors) and also changes (for instance, the introduction of connections to our whole-group read-alouds in the children's drawing and/or dictation and writing). Also, by Daniel's eighth visit, he had enough data to look back on and look for effective narrative points in his teaching as well as those he wanted to tinker with to strengthen the ongoing, evolving story of his work with the children.

Journals and Diaries—Telling a Story in Chronology

Journals and diaries also make use of text and images, and are effective narrative tools across the early childhood to elementary school span for documenting children's learning, for reflection, and for making instructional changes (Edwards & Rinaldi, 2009; Meier, 1997; Souto-Manning, 2006). Educators have long used journals and diaries to document their own teaching, to record their children's learning, and to reflect on their philosophies and educational dreams. One of the most well-known diaries in early childhood is *The Diary of Laura* (Edwards & Rinaldi, 2009), in which two infant teachers in one of the Reggio Emilia schools chronicle the discoveries and milestones of Laura, one of the infants in their care. *The Diary of Laura* is an aesthetically beautiful and personal account of Laura's learning and development, and includes her teacher's observations and insights in the text, which is complemented with simple and yet striking black and white photographs. By themselves the text and photographs each tell a story of Laura's development, and her teacher's reflections, together with the text and visuals create a compelling and instructive story of teaching, learning, and professional insight.

In elementary teaching, many educators have used journaling to make meaning of their practice, and some have later turned these journals into more public forms accessible to other educators. Magdalene Lampert, an elementary teacher and university professor, documented every day of her mathematics instruction in a fifth-grade class for one year, and the resulting analysis became *Teaching Problems and the Problems of Teaching* (2003), a book that brings to life the complex thinking processes that teachers use both minute by minute in the classroom and as they plan for teaching mathematics. Although Lampert has the advantage of research assistants and grant funding that allow her to collect and analyze far more data than many classroom teachers (e.g. copies of every page of every students' notebooks, a video record of every class session), she returns repeatedly to the centrality of her journal as a place to make meaning of what she encounters each day in the classroom. Her journaling shows the ways in which planning can move between the logistical, the intellectual, and the socio-emotional within the same thought. For instance, in her journal entry just before the start of the school year, she begins by noting the need to discuss room arrangement with her partner teacher, which leads to her questioning whether she wants the first day to focus on whole group discussion or on small group problem solving. While setting up the desks in a classroom may seem like the smallest of tasks to a non-educator, the thinking revealed in Lampert's journal allows us to see how the physical arrangement of the room and of students is completely tied to her instructional goals.

Journals, even irregularly kept as is often the reality for practicing teachers, allow us to remember and draw upon the story of a classroom over the course of a year. Teachers who engage in journaling as an ongoing practice are also able to compare the stories of different year's classes, noticing how what is wonderfully effective with one group of children must be tweaked or completely thrown out when a new cast of characters sit in those same chairs. Capturing a story as it unfolds over time allows us to revisit people and ideas in the ever changing classroom landscape, and to better understand how our successes and struggles came to be.

Journals with Families—Martha Melgoza

Martha Melgoza is a veteran early childhood educator who is currently the director/teacher of Skytown Parent Cooperative in Kensington, California, which features a play-based, emergent curriculum (Jones & Nimmo, 1994). Martha keeps a journal to reflect on her work as a director who also teaches alongside the school's teachers and the small group of parents who are participating during their designated "teaching" week. Martha uses her journal to find topics and prompts for the participating parents to "engage in a dialogue about children at a deeper level." Martha shares her journal prompt during the weekly Monday morning meeting for the parents participating during their week (a copy is emailed to those parents who have an "off" week). Martha wants the journal to facilitate discussion and reflection during the morning meeting, and at the end of each school day parents have time to ask or share what they observed, learned, or were frustrated by in regard to Martha's journal prompt. It is a form of collective storying (oral and written) of the children's learning and the adults' reactions and thoughts. Martha also integrates aspects of her journal in the weekly parent newsletter, which has addressed a range of topics—differences in children's language development, children's development through the lens of gender, children's interactions and conflict, and children as members of communities.

In one journal entry on children in communities, Martha reflects on intriguing connections between home and school for the children.

> While working with children one often hears stories from them about their experiences outside of school. It's interesting to think about how children encounter and are affected by different aspects of society.

In the same entry, Martha also includes narrative data from a parent group discussion about home-school connections.

> On Monday's end of day meeting Dia (parent) offered the example of Naava and Charlotte (children) seeing each other at a local library. They both were at the library because they have parents who have the interest and the time to bring them there. Being members of the same community made the meeting between the children exciting and memorable.

Martha also uses a multi-column format (Figure 3.10) for going "deeper" into the journaling and observation process. It helps Martha separate out her thoughts and affords some distance between reviewing her journal entries.

Martha follows certain guidelines that she has refined over the last several years: the first column covers the actual event with no interpretation, the second column is for the interpretation and connections to the curriculum, and the third column is for furthering her thoughts or ideas. The last two columns change as the need arises for variation.

The first column allows Martha to document and narrate small moments in the children's play and engagement ("Luc, Uli, Declan, and Shane playing a game. Nico in his firefighter game. Siren louder than usual. Nico keeps running over to the boys and telling them they need to be rescued."). The second column provides a snippet of the ongoing "reflection story" of Martha trying to understand underlying processes in the children's play ("The boys continued with their desire to play. I saw both sides attempting to make connections. Missed communication still happening. Support we have been providing for the communication does not appear to be taking root. Need to rethink."). The third column is a form of "meta story" that allows Martha to consider next steps in the evolution of the children's play and engagement ("All kids about the same age; share many interests; have grouped them together in hikes, same dynamic. It appears they want to play together. Yes? No? Bring up in staff meeting to see what others have observed."). Taken together, the three columns create a small story of Martha's documentation and reflections, and over time Martha's journal entries are an evolving collection of small moments, anecdotes, conversations, and insights that tell the story of the children's learning and the adults' reactions and insights.

Narrative-Based Letters

Letters are a little-used tool in narrative inquiry, though they have the potential to tell engaging stories of teaching and learning in an immediate, personal manner. Letters are a particularly open-ended genre of writing that lend themselves to storytelling, and to an interweaving of critical moments, incidents, and anecdotes

September 2, 2014 Original Entries	September 5, 2014 Review and Reactions	September 8, 2014 Further Connections and Insights
9:20 a.m. Alex working w/magnetic birds. Color coordinating the body parts	Looking to see what develops w/repeat exposure to magnet props.	Looked back at my goals and concepts and yes, this is what I am wondering—do they feel, talk about, or in any way notice the repel/ attract concept? Keep putting out activities. Look back at my magnet web.
10:20 a.m. Luc, Uli, Declan, and Shane-playing a game. Nico in his firefighter game. Siren louder than usual. Nico keeps running over to boys and telling them they need to be rescued ("There's a fire. You need to leave. It's dangerous.") The boys do not respond. They keep making Nico the bad guy ("Nico's the bad guy. Run!").	Does Alex notice the push/pull of the magnets?	
	The boys continued w/their desire to play together. I saw both sides attempting to make connection. Missed communication still happening.	All kids about the same age; share many interests; have grouped them together in hikes—same dynamic.
11:15a.m. Declan and Shane are playing on the slide with cars. They are sending the cars up the slide.	Support we have been providing for the communication does not appear to be taking root.	It appears they want to play together. Yes? No?
Shane: We can test it now	Need to re-think.	Bring up in staff meeting to see what others have observed.
Declan: Zoom them. Then he will fly.		
Kita: Look what I found (she just walks up to them with a car and tries to give it to them).		Go back and review ramps book for possible ideas to support.
		Look into other ramp materials to add to the outdoor pile.
12:30 p.m. Julio (snake) gets brought out and Kita and Hanna-Mae enjoy trying to create an obstacle course for him. Julio complies. Girls laugh.	Some of the kids have continued last year's car and ramp exploration. Interesting since neither of these boys was part of it back then.	They just let her in. They did not let Kallidin in at all. The threesome still of interest to me as well as the specific child rejection. Kallidin was just as thoughtful in attempt at entry yet no go.
Bennett and yoga.	Bennett participated in an activity. All the watching paid off. He had so much fun. Will send picture of it to his mom.	This was a spontaneous activity from end of day story yesterday.
Green monster book out again.		The kids were fascinated by the book even though they had heard it before. The concept of how it was put together is what they noticed.
	What fun we had with this. A good group of kids were part of it. Declan showed up at the art table!! And stayed awhile. Charlotte captured a big concept!	Charlotte followed the whole thought process as she pieced it together.

FIGURE 3.10 Martha's three-column journal entry.

that need no particular order or organization. Visuals, such as photographs and drawings, are also easily integrated into letters. Letters are also an especially effective form of narrative inquiry to promote social justice and equity, and for educators to feel passionate about sharing their ideas and feelings with others as a form of solidarity, persuasion, and dialogue. In this vein, letters can serve as counter-stories to dominant narratives that may impede teacher and student freedom, agency, and voice.

Mary Cowhey (2008), an elementary school teacher, wrote an impassioned letter to Paulo Freire, the legendary educational thinker and philosopher from Brazil who died in 1997. In her letter to Freire, Cowley writes about her experiences "reading" her classes as related to Freire's ideas on "reading the world," a process of critical analysis and consciousness to promote transformative and additive educational ideas and practices. Cowley uses her letter to recount key memories and incidents about her very first day of teaching, individual students who have had an impact on her, and books and stories that have helped her "read" her class and the arc of her teaching career.

READING THE CLASS
(Cowley, 2008)

I remember I showed my lesson plans to a more experienced first-grade teacher for her advice. She glanced at my plan, which included a morning meeting, a math lesson to introduce materials and assess students, a read-aloud of *Santiago*, a shared reading of *I Went Walking* with a dramatization and introduction of the pocket chart, and introduction of the ABC center, reading aloud a chapter of *My Father's Dragon* after lunch, a discussion of student goals . . . She cackled and said, "You're not really thinking you're going to *teach* the first day, are you?" I was so mad and embarrassed that I wanted to cry. My face burned. She walked out of my room still laughing at me. I went back to taping up Romare Bearden artwork from an old calendar over the coat hooks and thought, "Damn straight I'm going to teach the first day!"

The letter allows Cowley to traverse time and space and experience, revisiting telling moments and incidents that encapsulate some of Freire's key ideas that form the foundation for Cowley's teaching philosophy.

Drama and Reader's Theatre

The use of drama has a long history in education as a tool for teacher expression and for reaching multiple audiences in varied avenues and media.

Theatre of the Oppressed

The work of Paolo Freire has been popularized in the work of Augusto Boal's (1979) use of the Theatre of the Oppressed. Boal was interested in using drama to help participants move from a state of silence to action, a process that parallels Freire's ideas on transformative education. Boal's Theatre of Oppressed makes use of the human body and dialogue to tell the story of critical issues, ideas, feelings, and predicaments of the participants. Boal outlines four stages for this process of moving from silence to voice and action: (1) knowing the body (moving the body in ways that indicate social oppression and exclusion); (2) making the body expressive (moving the body in more movements); (3) the theatre as language (moving the body in varied ways in concert and in reaction to other participants); and (4) theatre as discourse (moving the body to express certain thoughts, themes, feelings). In the drama, according to Boal, "you discover yourself in what you do" (www.youtube.com/watch?v=y5cYAz6n4Ag), and learn to tell your own story of experience, dreams, and hopes.

Readers' Theatre

Just as readers' theatre is an effective instructional tool for increasing students' interest in and engagement with literary and nonfiction texts as emphasized with Common Core State Standards, readers' theatre has the potential for increasing teacher understanding and reflection on student learning and instruction. Readers' theatre can be carried out in varied media—oral/spoken word, written, drama, electronic media—and to reach varied audiences in more public and artistic ways than some other narrative forms. Rebecca Akin and Gerald Campano (2009), two elementary school teachers, edited a readers' theatre text featuring the voices and written excerpts from 20 K–12 teachers and administrators who told stories that examined professional resiliency and identity. Most of the excerpts were originally composed as part of teacher inquiry groups, and integrated into a cohesive script for presentation at a conference. The script is divided into four main parts: student portraits, questions, gender and race, and portraits of teachers and pedagogy. Each of these larger sections include stage directions ("Elizabeth stands at microphone #3. Maria stands at microphone #5.") and the excerpts spoken by the authors. For example, in the student portraits section, Maria Ghiso (a dual language kindergarten teacher) recounts small moments about writing:

> Writing is a way to share from your life, I tell my students. With them I write about traveling home to Argentina and how my grandmother used to make me *café con leche* and say it tasted so special because she used *leche de vaca negra*—milk from a black cow. In class Daniela writes about a visit from the *ratoncito*, the large rodent that is the Latin American version of the tooth fairy. Lenny only writes about Pokemon. Alejandra writes about playing mom in the housekeeping corner, and the baby is always sick with fever. (p. 348)

In the section on race and gender, Kelly Harper, a sixth-grade teacher, recalls moments of how race and gender intersect in children's literature:

> What happens when sixth graders in an affluent, almost all-White school community read children's literature specifically selected to address issues of race and diversity? At first, students were overwhelmingly positive. After reading *Card and Cwidder*, for example, Cassie commented: "I think that the author is making a point about the world today, and I think it's sad that people are always living in fear. This is a great story, though, and I look forward to reading what happens next." In the coming months, however, as our conversations got deeper, my students' receptivity levels shifted—growing enthusiasm for many, but emerging resistance for some. (p. 362)

Rebecca Akin and Gerald Campano argue that the use of the readers' theatre script provides a forum for "multiple representations of teaching side by side," which allows audiences to enter "a space where teaching is experienced as moving, changing, contradictory, and fluid" (p. 378). Readers' theatre, then, has the potential to tell parts of stories, bits and pieces of narrative, a moment here and an anecdote or memory there. These stories and narrative fragments can then coalesce into a well-formed, provocative medium for individual self-expression, communal solidarity, and reflection and change.

Using Multimedia Tools for Narrative Inquiry

Multimedia tools, such as video and blogging, are becoming increasingly popular techniques for taking a narrative stance to observing student learning, reflecting on the quality of one's teaching, and for sharing one's story with a wider audience of educators and others locally, nationally, and even internationally.

Video as a Narrative Tool

In her work as an elementary science teacher, Stephanie experimented with video as a means to focus on students' voice rather than her immediate inferences about their levels of understanding. In her ongoing narrative inquiry, she felt that she often struggled to capture the voice and stories of her students in ways that prioritize their own viewpoints rather than her own. On rereading narratives, she often found that the stories she captured presumed quite a lot about what a student was thinking, perhaps based more on Stephanie's inferences and her own experiences than on the students'. Even when engaged directly in one-on-one conversations, she knew that her status as the teacher could make students likely to say what they thought she wanted to hear rather than what might really be on their minds.

Several years ago, Stephanie began experimenting with "self interviews," in which she provided a written or spoken prompt, and individual children then went to a private spot in or near the classroom and videotaped themselves responding to the prompt. Interestingly, what students said when alone with the camera was often both qualitatively and quantitatively different than what they said in typical classroom conversation. These short videos have become not only an important part of Stephanie's classroom assessment practice, but also an important tool for narrative inquiry, as they provide students' stories of classroom life and content understanding from an entirely different vantage point, without the teacher at the center.

Consider, for example, the case of Sonya, a six-year-old who participated in a two-week-long summer science camp focused on the properties of plants as they are used by humans (for nutrition, medicine, and cloth dyeing, for example). As one of the daily centers from which students could freely choose, Stephanie set up a video interview station in a quiet room. Sonya chose to spend a few minutes there every day. She was a quiet, attentive child who seemed particularly drawn to the artistic aspects of our projects. At first, her video responses matched Stephanie's perception of her. For instance, on day three, she gave detailed descriptions of the mug she designed for testing herbal tea, with little mention of testing the properties of different teas. But on day five, her video interview revealed that she was fascinated with the pH testing the children had done of different herbal teas and other plant-based drinks, and she had a lot of questions and ideas. She said, "I wonder if the stuff in my stomach gets more acidy if I drink lemonade. Maybe I can eat faster if I drink lemonade with it." Stephanie followed up the next day, asking Sonya to tell me more about that idea, and she revealed a well-thought out theory that drinking low-pH (acidic) drinks would strengthen her stomach acid, which would make foods digest more quickly. As a result of Sonya's idea, which she only revealed aloud via the video interview, Stephanie worked with her and a few other children to design a test of how quickly different foods dissolved in acidic, neutral, and basic liquids.

Sonya's follow-up video interviews focused almost entirely on this newly developed project. She even began one video session with the words, "Here's the latest update on the acid project. You aren't going to believe this!" As she saw her story reflected in the camp's daily activities, she seemed to become more connected to the science itself.

Electronic Blogs—Telling Stories to Wider Audiences

Electronic blogs can make use of text, video, photographs, and other visuals in an appealing and readily sharable format. In this respect, blogs share certain similarities with other narrative techniques that meld text and visuals as discussed earlier in the examples above from Renetta Goeson and Michael Escamilla. Since educators often contribute separate entries over time, blogs also resemble diaries and journals such as discussed earlier in the examples from *The Diary of Laura* and the preschool director/teacher Martha Melgoza's work. As an online forum, though, they are also a form of public diaries accessible by larger and more distant audiences (McNeill, 2003; Nardi, Schiano, & Gumbrecht, 2004).

Blogs offer great flexibility in form and content for educators, who can write about and show visuals for a particular topic or project just once, or can return to the same topic or story over a period of time ranging from weeks to months. The opportunity for readers to respond to blog posts also adds another narrative layer, a side or compendium story in which readers carry on their own commentary and contribute their own experiences and stories as linked to the blog. Educators can author their own blog on their own, or contribute to a blog sponsored by their school or a professional organization or group. Blogs that are part of a group effort have the added dimension of contributing to a collaborative collection of educators' experiences and stories.

Telling Stories as a Whole School—Blogs from the Sabot Stony Point School

Sabot Stony Point School is a P–8, independent school in Richmond, Virginia, that encourages its faculty to contribute to a school-wide archive of blog posts. The blogs are an opportunity for teachers to tell the story of the school's philosophy and curriculum. Each year the school has a school-wide "umbrella project" for preschoolers to middle schoolers, and the blog posts function as an electronic forum for the teachers to contribute their students' work and learning, and their reflections on their teaching as linked to the school-wide project. The teachers also create a brief profile on the site, and can list other blogs that they follow. The teachers employ varied narrative inquiry strategies in their blogs, utilizing video, photographs, teacher-written text, and student play and work samples, and older students at the school post their own work within the teachers' blogs.

Andrea Pierotti—Grade 3 Blog Post

Third-grade teacher Andrea Pierotti created a series of posts (www. toputononesthinkingscap.blogspot.com/) chronicling her class's field trips to observe Richmond's bridges in preparation for curricular work on engineering. In one post, on October 29, 2015, Andrea posted 14 photographs, which show the students observing and sketching the bridges, and forming a community of observers and investigators of their local community. Like a journal entry, the blog allows Andrea to date her postings to show the chronology of the children's explorations (an earlier post showed a previous Richmond field trip). Andrea starts the story of the field trip by setting the scene and squarely placing herself, personally and professionally, in the context of the trip and the blog post.

> We took our first Richmond field trip today. It was THE most perfect beautiful fall day. We rode the city bus downtown to the river to investigate bridges in preparation for some engineering challenges. Days like these make me just fall in love—in love with my class, my co-teacher, with my

job and with my Richmond. I found that after last year I kept wanting to take my own babies to the same places I had taken my class so that my babies could have the same magical experiences. It seems to work.

The blog format also allows Andrea to tell the story of the field trip via photographs accompanied by brief and more extensive captions, which help tell a well-told and engaging story of the children's learning as well as Andrea's insights and reflections. For example, a brief caption to accompany a photo read as: "Sketching the Manchester Bridge. Noticing the arches." A longer caption accompanied a photo of two children sitting and sketching a bridge (Figure 3.11)—"Sketching the bridge with the railroad. Luckily a train came just as we got there and it stopped on the bridge for at least an hour. The cars were FULL of coal so it really helped put into perspective how sturdy the bridge really needed to be."

Andrea also included snippets of student dialogue ("The bridge isn't straight across. It is bent."), questions ("Eating lunch on Belle Isle. Who would ever know we were smack in the middle of a giant city?"), and students' observations ("We noticed lots of Xs in the structures we saw. 'They are supporting the supports,'

FIGURE 3.11 Two students sketching the bridge. [Photo credit: Andrea Pierotti]

one child said."). As Andrea's blog post shows, the reader can start anywhere in the post and then scroll up or down to play with the sequence of Andrea's "published" blog story. In effect, blog posts can function like picture books to be interpreted on multiple narrative levels.

Blogs also have similarities to chapter books, and feature installments of "what happened next" text and visuals. For instance, a month later, Andrea posted another post that describes and reflects on how she and her class have revisited their bridge trips. Andrea starts this post by setting the context and describing the provocation or puzzle to engage the children:

> It has been a mantra for years at Sabot [School] that "The story of one child is the story of all children," meaning that by focusing in on one learning experience helps us understand more about learners in general. I think it could also be said that the story of one bridge building group is the story of all bridge building groups. By telling the story of one group, we hope to highlight the type of thinking and work we see going on in all. While all groups' experiences are not identical, we see common threads of planning, building, testing, communicating, learning to let go and revising. We see each group needing to come to the question of what is best for their bridge. Below is a story of revision. One group was given the assignment to build a bridge that went from the bottom of a cliff up to the top. After working for a while, the group had finished their first version. As they tested it, they noticed that it wasn't really working very well. It wasn't very stable and it collapsed easily. The car also had to drive almost vertically to the top of the cliff.

Andrea again uses text (description, snippets of conversation, and analysis) and photographs to provide an update on the children's continuing engagement with design, collaboration, and studying their local environment and history. The photographs, much as they do in the other examples in this chapter, tell their own story of student engagement and productivity (Figure 3.12).

Andrea's blog posts, then, provide an online forum for documenting the children's own documentation, experimentation, dialogue, and collaboration. Her posts tell the essential tale of the small narrative points ("Within fifteen minutes they had a single span large") as well as some of the larger narrative threads of Andrea's teaching and reflection ("I think it could also be said that the story of one bridge building group is the story of all bridge building groups").

When Andrea first began blogging, she used the blog "to reflect on the steps we had taken as a learning community to arrive where we were. It was really by taking the time to document our process through pictures, quotes and storytelling that I began to get the rhythm of project work. I began to see larger patterns and know what to expect even if the projects weren't exactly the same" (A. Pierotti, personal communication, February 1, 2016). Andrea has found increased value in

FIGURE 3.12 Within 15 minutes they had a single span large enough to reach floor to cliff. Light. Strong. Stable. [Photo credit: Andrea Pierotti]

the blogs over time as her posts tell more stories, more deeply, about her class's field trips and their related activities. She now sees that the blog allows her "to step back and look for bigger ideas," and the blogging has become "a form of teacher meditation, to have a place to share valuable moments or ask big questions." The blog format has also provided new narrative techniques for Andrea to tell her teaching stories, as she can use "video, sound, pictures, transcripts of conversations or quotes" with her reflections, and "the dynamic nature of the blog seems more fitting for the dynamic types of thinking and collaborating" that Andrea and her class are engaged in. Last, Andrea has found that the public nature of her multimedia-based blogging widens the audiences for her stories, and validates her teaching and the children's learning. Andrea "can show the images of the thoughtful things" her students created, and "show video of their passionate negotiations, and "share transcripts of their responsive conversations with each other." Moving forward, as Andrea recounts more stories of her teaching via blogging, she hopes that the posts "change the way the world views" her students, and that "the stories show the world that children can think when given the space" and how through "storytelling new possibilities for education come to light."

Collaboration Across Schools—Blogs from the Mills Teacher Scholars

The Mills Teacher Scholars in Oakland, California, is a network for Mills College graduates and other local teachers conducting classroom-based research and inquiry. The teachers meet on a regular basis at their individual sites to discuss their ongoing inquiry work, and also meet as a whole network at a once-a-year Scholars event, where teachers present their inquiry work in a panel format. The teachers' inquiry work is also posted in blog format on the network's website (http://millsscholars.org/), and regular emails to network teachers and others disseminate new blog postings. The archived blog postings serve as a repository for the teachers' inquiry work, and the blog postings offer the opportunity for teachers to tell critical incidents, experiences, perspectives, activities, and findings from their projects. The blogs make use of text and visuals and allow for electronic comments from other network members and the general public.

Emily Starr Bean's Blog—Creative, Courageous Writing in Kindergarten

Emily teaches in a dual immersion, Spanish/English kindergarten classroom at Melrose Leadership Academy in the Oakland Unified School District, which is a project-based school focusing on a single topic for several months. In her inquiry work, Emily looked at her students' daily creative writing journals, discussed their writing with the children, and had informal conversations with the children's families about their writing. In her blog post (http://millsscholars.org/creative-courageous-writing-in-kindergarten/), Emily discusses her main discoveries about her children's writing (under the umbrella term of "creative, courageous writing") and posts examples of her students' journal entries that illustrate particular qualities of their writing and Emily's instructional strategies.

As a public forum, Emily's blog received a response from a teacher in a neighboring district, who shared about the pressures of teaching writing to young children, and how Emily's emphasis on drawing validated the responder's own work with her students' writing development. Emily views blogs as a form of professional storytelling that offers important benefits for teachers' teaching and professional growth (E. S. Bean, personal communication, 11 January 2016) in these critical ways:

- create a "space" to document professional work
- communicate teachers' knowledge to fellow educators, the school community, and a broader audience
- develop "professional networks of support and share best practices"
- promote "institutional memory" for teachers' inquiry and reflections so they don't "disappear"
- provide a forum for including families in the classroom
- make public the "intentionality" of teachers' work and the "thoughtfulness driving our decisions"

Emily argues that blogs "shift the narrative around teachers and rather than being spoken for or about, we can speak for ourselves and begin to rewrite the story being told." The dominant narratives of educational reform over the last 30 years "often fail to illuminate the stories that create the realities of the day-to-day life in classrooms." For Emily, storytelling in the form of a blog is a transformative way to "humanize" her work and that of her colleagues, and to avoid the societal image of teachers as "reduced to numbers and standards."

Emily strongly believes that by engaging in the inquiry structure provided by the Mills Teacher Scholars (selecting an inquiry question, examining student work, refining the question, re-examining student work, shifting teacher practice, and examining the work again), "a story is bound to unfold." The process of the blog writing, and the selection of student writing samples, challenged Emily "to make sense of the data, understand the learning process, and find possible holes in the story" she had discovered. The form and function of an electronic blog, then, allow Emily to share the successes of her teaching with a larger audience, and to validate for herself the strength of her teaching, and to give voice and celebrate the academic achievements of her young students.

Closing—Putting Narrative Tools into Practice

This chapter has described several tools for using narrative inquiry to understand student learning and engagement, inform one's teaching, share one's teaching ideas and passions with colleagues and the wider community, and contribute to one's professional growth and development. It is important to select those narrative tools that feel most comfortable and "doable" for you—what makes good logistical sense for you and your teaching context. You might, if the narrative tools are mostly new and unfamiliar for you, try out one or two tools that appear most likely to maximize your "narrative success" at the outset of a teaching activity or inquiry project. For instance, starting a teaching journal might be a good place to begin—creating a brief entry each week for several weeks makes for a doable beginning, and will most likely result in several possible narrative threads that one can pursue later in more detail and depth via the inclusion of other narrative tools. For those more experienced with some of the narrative tools discussed in this chapter, it might be beneficial to combine a few tools at the same time. For instance, gathering material and then creating a series of blog posts makes use of an innovative electronic medium and allows one to integrate narrative-based text and photographs that tell a teaching and learning story. For those of you with a great deal of experience with narrative and inquiry, you might also pursue work in video, which can be shared with your students, colleagues, and families for discussion and next steps, and also posted online for further dialogue with a larger audience locally, nationally, and internationally.

At some future point, after trial and error on one's own, it can be beneficial to include students, families, colleagues, and even community members in the selection and use of certain narrative inquiry tools. In this respect, we expand the narrative circles of inquiry and others become co-inquirers and co-storytellers around a particular project, idea, product, trip, or idea. Our stories as educators are often enlivened and deepened through the inclusion of others' voices, ideas, feelings, experiences, and stories. They can keep us honest, keep our biases in check, and expand the horizons of our understanding, knowledge, and awareness of curriculum, teaching, and philosophies that drive our teaching and improve our schools. Including others can keep our stories "honest" and accountable to others' perspectives and needs and talents, and it indicates to outside audiences that their stories count, too, and have a trustworthiness that we value and cherish as inquiring, curious individuals and community members.

4

TELLING SOMEONE ELSE'S STORY

Narrative Inquiry for Understanding Individual Children

Early childhood teachers often work in classrooms of a dozen or more children, and in the elementary years, the number of students in a single teacher's classroom can climb above 30. So it is not at all surprising that classroom teachers are often hesitant to restrict their research to a single child or even to a small group. Alina Gish, whose research into effective social emotional curricula for first graders is profiled in Chapter 2 (Gish, 2015), illustrates this dilemma well. She taught in a first-grade classroom with 18 students, and she was implementing a newly adopted whole-class, whole-school curriculum. Initially, she logically assumed that the strongest research approach would be to collect data on all of her students, to look for changes that might correlate to the new curriculum, and to use measures such as counts of target behaviors and pre- and post-tests from all students as direct measures of the program's impact. This is a widely used approach to direct teacher research, and in many cases collecting and analyzing this data gives teachers valuable insights into what is and is not working for the class as a whole.

Alina quickly encountered several problems with her design. First and perhaps most urgently, she realized she could not possibly gather accurate data on the behaviors of 18 students at once. She tried to address this by videotaping target lessons, but this left her with hours and hours of videotape that would take a research team months to accurately code in the way Alina originally planned. She realized this was not only impossible given all the other demands of teaching, but also wouldn't provide her with "just in time" knowledge to help her current students in their current situations. Additionally, as much as she wanted to focus on everyone at once, she realized that her observers' eye, not to mention much of her teaching energy, was being primarily directed toward two students, "Roger" and

"John." Tally marks of behaviors were not accurately capturing what was going on with these students. The constant interruptions, the intense teacher/student interactions, the times that one or both students had to be removed from the rest of the class, all of these things weighed on Alina's mind, and she realized that even though she wanted to know about how the whole class experienced the curriculum, what she *needed* to know was more about the stories of these two boys for whom neither the curriculum nor school in general seemed to be a "good fit," even in the early months of first grade.

Alina's decision to radically shift her project and focus on fully capturing Roger's story (and later, John's as well), did not sit well with her at first. Teachers know that it is their responsibility to reach all of their students, and the decision to focus a project on only one or two can feel selfish or even irresponsible. This is especially true when the chosen focal child already seems to take up more than his or her fair share of the teacher's time and brain space. And yet, as Alina discovered, the switch from all-encompassing data to uncovering individual narratives can have repercussions beyond the single child. As she explored Roger's and John's stories more fully, the first thing she began to realize was the extent to which she had grouped them together as "problem children," to the point that she was at first unaware of John's slow but certain adoption of age-appropriate social behaviors. Her gut feeling that the curriculum did not work for children whose behaviors were far outside the norm was challenged by her growing understanding of the counter-narrative that John provided. Additionally, while the school year ended without many outward signs of progress for Roger, she found many puzzling aspects of his story that challenged her assumptions about him, including his near perfect score on the official post-assessment for the social emotional curriculum.

When we begin work to uncover the stories of a single child, we find that the complexity of this work often requires us to narrow our focus. When we try to collect everyone's stories at once, not only is the task overwhelming, but we are also prone to pull out the pieces of the stories that match what we already believe to be true. We can also use the sheer volume of data as a sort of wall that prevents us from connecting our own teacher narratives with those of our students. If we instead work to fully tell the story of a single child, we must come to terms with the fact that his or her story is not ours, and that it may contradict the narrative we have invented about them to explain the parts of the child we do not yet understand. Conversely, knowing someone else's story means knowing that person as a network of relationships and experiences (Clandinin, 2013). As we build a more complete narrative of a child, even though it is bounded in time and place, we build connections between the child, his or her broader world, and necessarily, ourselves.

In this chapter, we take up both the promises and the challenges of engaging in narrative inquiry that has children's stories as the focus. While it is certainly important to tell our own stories as teachers in relationship with children, colleagues, and curriculum, it is vital that we also seek to gather and make meaning of the stories of children. Without them, we work in a world of assumptions and one-sidedness, unable to check our beliefs and versions of truth that guide our practice.

Observation, Inference, and The Challenges of Telling Someone Else's Story

---

CHAYA IN SCIENCE CLASS (FIFTH GRADE)

Stephanie Sisk-Hilton

Silence again. Chaya seems to be able to sense when my ears attend to her voice, even when I work hard to neither turn my body toward her nor indicate in any way that I am paying attention to her. When she sits with LoAnn, Marisol, and Lai, her body visibly relaxes, and I see her mouth moving, clearly saying something to her friends. And only in this group does she step out of her self-appointed role of recorder, only because Lai is a quicker and more fluent writer. So Lai holds the marker, and Chaya leans forward, pointing to the chart paper, suggesting, I assume, things to add to their growing list of what might cause illnesses. And yet when I edge closer, facing and pretending to listen in on the table group across from them, she goes silent. I glance behind me, and she sat back fully in her chair, head down. She will speak to me only in polite, short responses to direct questions (and often even those are sometimes met with a downward look and a shrug), and she goes silent even when I am merely within 10 feet of her. What is going on in her mind that makes her so afraid of me?

Chaya was one of the students in the fifth-grade class with whom Stephanie first engaged in narrative inquiry. She was an unlikely choice of focal student for this approach, given that, as shown in the data segment above, Chaya rarely spoke in the presence of adults—especially, it seemed, Stephanie. But the issue that kept Stephanie up at night during that school year was how stereotypical and gendered the participation patterns were among this group of students. This group of students had been together as a class in fourth grade as well, so their norms were well established, but Stephanie was new to the school and was completely flummoxed by this classroom's culture. A group of about five boys were by far the heaviest participators in classroom talk, and they spoke with such authority (and frequency) that other students seemed to defer to their expertise. A group that represented almost a majority of the class, about half of the boys and three or four of the girls, participated when called on and worked eagerly in small groups, especially when their group did not contain one of the dominant talkers. And then there were the silent girls. Six girls in the class, five of them from the same Southeast Asian tribal group, rarely spoke in class. Most would respond to direct teacher questions, and all of them otherwise participated in the life of the class, completing assignments and seeming to listen when others spoke. All of them had developed the habit of taking on the "recorder" role in small groups, even when it was initially assigned to someone else. They seemed to use the act of writing what others' said as a way to legitimately participate in the group without engaging in conversation. Other students accepted and encouraged this by handing over the marker to one of these girls as soon as work groups formed.

Chaya was the most extreme example of a "silent girl." She rarely spoke at all in class, whether in whole or small group, to other students or to the teacher. When Stephanie looked at her, she shifted her gaze downward. While she would respond to a direct question from Stephanie, she looked terribly uncomfortable whenever she asked her to speak. So when Stephanie started her narrative inquiry into issues of participation in this class, she decided to focus on the stories of three participants: the highest of the high talking boys, herself as the teacher, and Chaya.

As the weeks progressed, this plan seemed ill advised. Because Chaya revealed so little about herself, the narratives Stephanie initially collected took two forms. In one, she wrote about Chaya's actions, but those tended to be brief, since Chaya nearly stopped moving when Stephanie looked her direction. The other form of narrative was not really about Chaya at all, but was instead Stephanie's filtering of Chaya's actions through the lens of her own story.

STEPHANIE THINKS ABOUT CHAYA

I wonder if I am scaring her. I so often feel like the loud New Yorker in this school full of gentle, California talking teachers who end every sentence sounding like a question. Sometimes the gentle talk makes me want to scream. Which I'm guessing is not the best attitude to project to a child who is already afraid to talk.

I am scared of so many things, but talking isn't one of them. Words have always been the way I make meaning of life, the one thing I have complete control over. I choose what comes out of my mouth, what comes out of my pen. As a kid, when we played "would you rather," I always, always chose blind over deaf or mute. And later, in high school, when Ms. G. looked at me disparagingly and commented, "You sure talk more than [your older sister]," I took it as a badge of honor rather than the insult she intended. And in college I ditched my southern accent so my words would be taken more seriously.

These stories of Stephanie's own life revealed part of why she was struggling so to understand Chaya's positioning. In Stephanie's world, words held power, and choosing not to use them was giving up one's power to tell one's own story. She could only imagine deep trauma or tyranny as a reason to give up words. She did not have an alternative story, and so Stephanie made things up about Chaya's story based on Stephanie's own life experience.

This tendency to infer from our own experience when we do not understand someone's story is a key danger in engaging in narrative inquiry from only the point of view of the teacher. Of course, the view of the researcher imbues all of the stories that she collects, but the more she focuses on fully understanding others' stories, the less she must rely on her own as the complete and unquestioned truth. Without a counter-narrative, Stephanie had a limited number of explanations for Chaya's silence: fear, trauma, differing cultural norms. These were the things that would silence Stephanie, but she had no evidence that these explained Chaya's silence.

Stephanie's observational stories initially backed up her working theory that she was frightening Chaya. At recess, Chaya played with friends, running around the play area in big games of tag, stopping to huddle with another girl under the play structure, heads together, seemingly talking. When Stephanie created a small group of only quiet girls, as in the narrative above, Chaya seemed more willing to talk, as long as Stephanie was not too nearby. So Stephanie was able to make her theory fit the limited evidence she had.

Then Stephanie had an idea for getting closer to Chaya's real story. One of her colleagues, Hattie, had been Chaya's second-grade teacher at a different school. One day, Stephanie walked by Hattie's classroom after school and, to her astonishment, Chaya and two other girls from Stephanie's class were inside, eagerly chatting with Hattie and helping her cut out paper shapes for a lesson. When the girls left, Stephanie went back to Hattie's room and asked her, "Does Chaya speak to you regularly? Did she speak in second grade?" Hattie confirmed that Chaya was very quiet but said that she would never think of her as silent. She did, in fact, regularly stop by Hattie's classroom after her younger students were gone, and she always spoke.

Stephanie asked Hattie if she would come observe in her class and try to figure out what was going on. She agreed and came several times over the next few weeks, observing Chaya and the other girls, and eventually interviewing her, something Stephanie had tried unsuccessfully several times. As Stephanie listened to Hattie's emerging findings, a new, tentative story emerged:

A REFLECTION ON SILENCE

Maybe *not* talking is power, too.
In a classroom full of words,
Loud voices jockeying for position

Listen to me! Listen to me!
She does not jump in
Her work is always done
Eyes always listening
No one can find fault,
Even the loud grown up who wants to insist that she use her words.
Her words are not for someone else
To demand.

The stories of the silent girls revealed themselves only slowly to Stephanie, and they weren't at all what she expected. Over two years, she worked to understand their classroom lives by inviting them to tell their own stories, by asking colleagues like Hattie to connect with them, and gradually by checking her own emerging ideas with them directly. She learned that while some of their stories involved fear and notions that "good girls" were to remain silent, none of them seemed to feel powerless in the classroom, as she had assumed. She also learned that they and others felt that only declarative statements "counted" as classroom participation. This revelation was critical as Stephanie worked to develop methods to elicit and value many types of classroom dialogue. She worked on giving more and explicitly valuing the asking of questions, not necessarily the authoritative answering of them. She invited dialogue that involved no spoken words through graffiti walls and silent "chalk talks." Stephanie's goal shifted from a single minded focus on equal "talk time" in the classroom toward finding ways to have a "voice" that did not always involve long sessions of spoken words.

As shown in the interactions of Stephanie with the "silent girls," using narrative to tell the story of another is a tricky business. Especially in a classroom setting, where the teacher/researcher acts within a deeply entwined relationship with her students, it can be difficult to tell the difference between a child's story and the teacher's own story as filtered through her assumptions about the child. Several techniques can help identify what is a representation of the child's own story, and what is not.

Tell The Story Without Emotion Words

When writing narratives about children in the classroom, it is often easy for teachers to assume we know not only *what* they are doing, but *why*. Consider the following segment from a teacher journal entry that Stephanie wrote quickly after class one day (in the middle of a science unit on asthma and the respiratory system).

RESPIRATORY SYSTEM POSTER

Version One

Why is [Chaya] so frightened all the time? Jared and Arun took over the group as they always do, talking with each other as though Chaya was not there. Leila jumped in occasionally, and it helped that she went to get the anatomy book to show everyone the alveoli and then would not let go of the book. Chaya began to make the group poster, but when Jared grabbed the paper and turned it toward him to begin drawing, Chaya shrunk back, lowered her head, and let him take over her typical role.

In her journal entry, Stephanie uses fear to interpret what she saw Chaya doing in the group. Even terms such as "took over" make assumptions about the children's intent based on the teacher's ideas about why people behave in certain ways. Consider now this second version, in which Stephanie works to write a narrative account of the same event:

RESPIRATORY SYSTEM POSTER

Version Two

Chaya starts out with the blue marker. She writes "How Blood Gets Oxygen" at the top of the page as Jared and Arun discuss where the alveoli are. Arun says they are on the outside of the lungs and move, carrying oxygen around. Jared says no, they are inside the lungs, and they get the oxygen into the blood, but only the blood moves. Leila jumps up from the table and says, "Hold on a sec." She returns with a book and flips through the pages to a drawing of the respiratory system. She directs everyone to look at the picture, and all four of them lean over the book. Chaya briefly traces her finger over part of the picture. Jared seems to read for a minute and then says, "See, I told you!" and reads an excerpt from the page. Chaya has returned to the poster, making a border around the outside. Jared says, "Hold on, we have to draw it" and pulls the poster toward him, flipping it around. Chaya keeps hold of her marker and sits back in her chair. Her head bows down. She looks over toward Leila's book, and Leila moves it slightly so it is between them.

The differences between the two accounts are clear when considered side by side. In the first, Stephanie is reflecting on her own experience witnessing the children's interaction. In the second, she is recording all of the details she can remember of what she saw happening, working to eliminate her assumptions about *why* it happened. The second moves from personal reflection to narrative account of observed actions.

The importance of trying to capture what we see and to separate it, in a sense, from our inferences, is methodologically important, but it is also narratively important. Narrative inquiry accepts as a given that all stories are "biased," and version two of the respiratory system narrative is not entirely unbiased. Of course, all narratives are by nature biased in some way, as what we choose to attend to, name, and write about depends upon our values and the problems or puzzles we have chosen to explore. Rather, the second narrative tries to tell the story in a way that leaves open many interpretations of meaning. The second telling still read to Stephanie like a story governed by fear of speaking. When she brought this narrative to a group of colleagues in a teacher inquiry group, though, they each focused on different aspects of the story, filtered through their own stories and narratives. One teacher expressed anger at Jared's taking over the situation and called him a "bully." Another was excited at how Leila had sought out additional research without teacher direction. And a third colleague said that he really liked the back and forth of actions and leadership among the group members, and said he didn't think the small "power moves" that others focused on were problematic. The version two narrative, still filtered through Stephanie's eyes and words, allowed others to make meaning of it in vastly divergent ways. In so doing, this made clear to Stephanie that she did not have a solid understanding of Chaya's story, and knowing that she did not know widened her inquiry path.

When we try to understand and record the narrative of someone's experience other than our own, we may not focus on what they find to be most important. We may capture details of what they say and do that hold deep meaning for the teacher/researcher, but that the person whose story we are telling finds insignificant. Allowing them to tell their own story is perhaps the most effective way to address this. But when we are working from our own observational notes, checking to see that we are retelling what we know happened, and not our assumed *whys*, allows us to examine the story for alternate meanings, insights, and puzzles.

How Children Tell Their Own Stories

Consider the difference between these two prompts, "What's it like to be sick?" and "Tell me a story about a time you were sick." Both might elicit interesting and meaningful responses. However, it is possible to answer the first one with single words: "yucky," "uncomfortable," "scary." But inviting a child to tell a story requires him to construct a narrative; to decide what is important to tell; and to have a beginning, a middle, and an end. Young children often love the invitation to tell a story, especially one about themselves. Older children, more aware of others' judgment and perhaps puzzled by a non-school-like request, may be more hesitant to jump in. But when we make inviting children's stories a regular part of our practice as teachers, we gather a trove of data into how our students think, what they remember most, and what they value most deeply.

When Stephanie was teaching Chaya's class, she was continuously puzzled by their behaviors, which often differed dramatically from other children she had taught. Stephanie had recently relocated from New York City to the San Francisco Bay Area, and she found that not only were her new students racially and culturally different than her previous students, but the cultural norms around schooling enacted by teachers at her school were different than her own. She was frustrated that her assumptions about students and how to motivate them proved inaccurate, and she realized that her stories of teaching and learning, and probably of life more broadly, were clashing with her students' and colleagues' stories.

Nervously, she decided to spend more time eliciting her children's stories. She made a goal of doing at least one "storytelling" lesson each week, gathering children's narratives in their own words. Sometimes these took the form of curriculum related "chalk talks," in which students grabbed markers and graffitied on chart papers headed with prompts such as (for their human body systems unit): "Memories of Being Sick / I remember . . . " and "Memories of Someone I Love Being Sick / I remember . . . " In math, she changed her reflection prompts so that every couple of weeks the prompt was "A Story of My Math Learning." She also tried less curricular prompts such as "What is a story from this week that you want to remember?" and "What does your teacher need to know about you right now?" Interestingly, the latter prompts only elicited in-depth responses from a few children in the first year. These fifth graders seemed more comfortable responding to prompts that were clearly about the topics they were studying, perhaps because the broader prompts did not match their ideas of what one does in school.

Sometimes the demands of writing get in the way of children telling their own stories. This is of course true of young children who do not yet know how to write, but it is also an issue with fluent writers who may find the task of recording a story in writing to be a chore. Sometimes the teacher can serve as the recorder for children, adding a caption to a picture or writing in details that are missing due to endurance rather than lack of story. Preschool and kindergarten teachers tend to do this as a regular part of their practice, but sometimes teachers of older children forget that offloading writing duties can be a real help to older children as well. Luckily, we also live in an age in which technology makes this an easy problem to address. Hitting "record" on one's smartphone after asking a child a narrative-eliciting question makes capturing the story as easy as listening to it. In elementary classrooms where one-on-one time with children may be very limited, a video or audio recording station can be set up in the corner of a classroom, and children can go there to tell their stories.

It is important to address an ethical issue in seeking to uncover and tell the stories of the children in our classroom as a part of our inquiry. In unstructured classroom moments, children often reveal parts of their story that a teacher could never collect through more formal means. A preschooler at the block center may interrupt building a skyscraper to tell the story of moving to a new apartment and being scared of the thumping sounds of feet overhead. A third grader on the playground may tell her friends the story of her high school sister braiding her hair for hours on Sunday afternoon while giving her insights into the world of teenage girls. These stories are gold for teacher researchers engaging in inquiry about the lives of children. However, ethically, we must use caution in mining them as data. If we were not meant to hear an exchange, it does not belong in our notes. Of course, overheard stories help us understand who children are and the lives they lead, and they may show up in our own reflective stories. But part of being an ethical researcher (and teacher) is only telling the stories we have permission to tell.

One way to address this ethical dilemma is to actively engage children in the narrative inquiry process. Beyond merely eliciting their stories for we as researchers to use as data, we can invite children to become our co-researchers, making meaning not only from their own stories but from those of others as well. For those working with younger children especially, this can at first sound like an impossibility. Narrative inquiry as a research methodology is difficult and time consuming. Finding patterns and core ideas in the messy stories of classroom life can be a slow process that involves a cycle of continuous rereading, more data collection, attempts at synthesis, and then a return to more data collection. But giving children access to stories of classroom life can wield new insights even to older and more skilled researchers.

As part of a research project looking at how young children determine importance during open ended science projects, she gave the children, ages five to nine, the option of recording brief "self interviews" each day after the daily project time. She said they could talk about what had been most important in the day's work or what they were wondering about. In the middle of the second week, she asked the children who had been making use of the video station if she could share some of their videos. During a whole group discussion, she showed video segments from each child who had agreed. She asked the group to listen for important ideas and for things that might be missing. Some of the reflections that came out in response to the video data included:

> Gabriel (age 9): I noticed that mostly everyone talked about the projects they invented themselves. Like if you spend a whole day or maybe a week making your own idea, you want to talk about it. But if it's something where you're following the directions, maybe it's really interesting, but maybe you don't really need to talk about it to the video.

Sonya (age 6): It's fun to just sit and you can talk and say what you think. Everyone looks kind of serious but kind of happy too. Like I looked serious but it was fun to do it.

Tia (age 8): Pretty much everyone talked about the project time. In [closing circle] we mostly talk about the games and stuff, but in the videos it's about the projects. I think maybe the projects are the most important things, but the games are the most fun things.

In this brief conversation about a small set of other students' reflections, children generated several possible explanations for what people chose to talk about and what they deemed "important." Tia made a distinction between "important" and "fun," and Sonya looked for evidence of how people were feeling about the very act of doing the self-interview, using herself as a reference point. All of their comments showed an attempt to understand a piece of another person's story, an attempt to make meaning based on the evidence in front of them. And while not particularly deep or complete on their own, this opportunity to *turn toward* the stories of others and integrate them with their own, engages children in their own inquiry rather than keeping them solely as subjects of it. Additionally, giving children control over whether or not to share their reflections handed over some of the power typically held by the researcher, an idea we take up more in the next section.

What Happens When We Focus on Someone Else's Story?

Teachers' narrative inquiries are often focused on themselves, on reflecting on their own stories in relation to children, curriculum, colleagues, and out-of-school lives. This is an important process in becoming a reflective and thoughtful educator. But when we broaden our inquiry to trying to learn and tell the stories of the children in our classroom, in relation to but separate from our own, several transformations may begin.

Learning someone else's story challenges the absolute truth of our own narrative. All of us bring to teaching assumptions about children in general as well as specific children based on their race, social class, parental temperament toward us, and a host of other features. Immersing ourselves in the search for stories around different aspects of our students' lives in and out of school inevitably lead to confronting some of these assumptions and truths. We become aware of limitations we are placing on children based not on their own characteristics but on our own.

On Losing and Gaining Power

The move toward narrative gathering as a research methodology and core classroom practice also requires teachers to give up some parts of their power in the classroom, namely the power to be the primary teller of the story. The writer Chimamanda Ngozi Adichie talks about being a child in Nigeria and writing stories in which her characters had blue eyes and played in the snow, since that was what the characters in the books she read looked like and did, even though she and everyone around her was brown eyed, and she had never seen snow. She says:

> What this demonstrates, I think, is how impressionable and vulnerable we are in the face of a story, particularly as children. Because all I had read were books in which characters were foreign, I had become convinced that books by their very nature had to have foreigners in them and had to be about things with which I could not personally identify. (Adichie, 2009)

Likewise, in schools, teachers often enact the dominant stories of how different children are expected to behave, interact, and learn in school, and they send both implicit and explicit messages to students that they need to join the story in progress, not tell their own. Narrative inquiry with children's stories at the center allows teachers to disrupt this system, sending a powerful message that children's stories hold power and meaning. When we work to learn and understand children's stories, even when we do not explain to children what we are doing, our actions are likely to change the power dynamic in our classrooms. If we are brave enough to engage children as co-inquirers, knowingly giving their stories and also struggling to make meaning of them in relation to others, we have the possibility of transforming our classrooms into spaces in which children and adults continually make, remake, and question meaning in relation to others.

Although we must give up the power that comes from owning one dominant story in order to engage in narrative inquiry based on the stories of our students, focusing on the intertwined stories of the people and relationships in our classrooms brings with it a new kind of power, the power to own our own story as part of what matters in the classroom. In the "silent girls" inquiry, Stephanie first struggled to learn the stories of Chaya and the other girls whose actions she did not understand. But in doing that, she also needed to tell her own story, both as part of her research process and as part of her teaching practice. She began writing about her own experiences growing up in a place where loud, opinionated girls were not generally appreciated in public spaces, and how she learned to navigate and challenge that world. Her pride in being someone who did not act like a "typical girl" was an important part the persona she brought with her to the classroom. As part of the inquiry process, she began to share pieces of her own childhood story with her students, just as she asked them to share their stories. Her students' stories challenged her idea that her own journey was a necessary one for all girls in a still inequitable society. But revealing this challenge aloud to her students began to gradually reduce the constant feeling of struggle she experienced whenever she tried to engage the class in conversation. The process of narrative inquiry nudged her teaching practice away from the notion of trying to "fix" the behaviors of her students toward engaging in relationship and the creation of shared meaning in classroom practices.

Facing Uncomfortable Truths

When the narratives that emerge through the inquiry process do not match the stories we have made up to explain things that trouble us, the result can be heart-wrenchingly uncomfortable. Sometimes "hard data," seemingly self-explanatory, is easier to look at than stories that clash with deeply held beliefs.

Consider, for example, the popular idea that children whose parents "care more" about them do better in school. The corollary to this belief is the idea that when children are struggling in school, particularly behaviorally, it is because the parents do not care enough to make the child a more compliant member of a teacher's classroom. In our combined 30 years working with teachers in training, we, the two authors, have found some version of these two beliefs to be nearly universal. From the vantage point of time, experience, and hundreds of pre-service teachers having passed through our classrooms, we know that this narrative of "parents don't care enough" is most rampant in situations in which the teacher and the students come from significantly different cultural, racial, or class backgrounds. As with most tightly held but unexamined beliefs, however, it is very difficult to get people to consider alternatives that explain children's unexpected behaviors more accurately than lack of parental care.

One year, Stephanie decided to use a brief cycle of narrative inquiry to take on this belief. She asked a group of student teachers to try to have five-minute conversations with the parent of every "problem child" in their class. She asked them to try to structure it as a friendly, informal conversation with the stated goal of a new teacher getting to know his or her students rather than as an official conference. They were not to bring up any complaints about the students' behavior, schoolwork, or homework during the conversation, but were instead to focus on getting to know the parent as a person. Each time the student teachers had a conversation, they spent a few minutes in class writing a narrative account of the conversation. For several weeks, no class time was spent discussing these conversations, just recording the narratives. Eventually, Stephanie asked students to spend some time reading all of the narratives they had collected. She then asked if anyone had found a parent who did not care about their child. The student teachers sat uncomfortably. One of them raised her hand and said there were several parents she was unable to talk to because they were never at the school to drop off or pick up their children. She said of course she knew they (probably) loved their children, but they didn't care enough about school to "be there" for them. Stephanie asked if there might be another possible story to explain the behaviors of these parents. Sitting in front of their collected mini-stories, students were quick to offer alternative stories: the parents might be working inflexible hours and could not get off work to take children to and from school; the parents might be scared of the teachers because they had bad experiences in school themselves; they might live far away and rely on the bus to transport children to and from school. Interestingly, the person who had not had conversations with the parents remained unconvinced that any story other than the "don't care" story explained the behavior of the parents or their children. It was students who had heard the stories of the parents they had labeled uncaring who were able to come up with and truly consider alternate explanations in which parents cared a lot, and children still misbehaved.

Engaging in narrative always requires the researcher to find holes in the story as known at any point in time and to elicit more information to more completely tell the story. Using narratives of children's (and perhaps their parents') experiences often involves moments in which the story we learn does not match the story we believe. Confronting inaccurate or unproductive beliefs is difficult, and our brains avoid it whenever possible (Nyhan, Reifler, & Ubel, 2013; Hart & Nisbet, 2011). But committing to the process of narrative inquiry can gradually make us, as both teachers and researchers, more comfortable with the uncertainty or incompleteness of our beliefs about teaching and learning, children and their families, and the role of schooling in children's lives.

5

NARRATIVE INQUIRY AS A SUPPORT FOR CURRICULAR INNOVATION

Teachers are in a constant cycle of developing, trying, assessing, and revising curriculum. We may spend the whole summer developing a new unit and be certain that it will be perfect for the students we have not yet met. Or we may be told that we must implement a new math curriculum, regardless of what we think of it, because the school district has adopted it and we will be assessed on how well students perform using it. Even in a more open-ended, emergent environment, we may carefully gather materials that we imagine children will use in a certain way. Whatever the impetus, when we implement a new curriculum or introduce new materials or structures to the classroom environment, we begin the process with preconceived ideas about how things will go and how children will respond.

When we introduce the new curriculum to children, these preconceived ideas will impact what we notice in terms of how children respond, a phenomenon known as confirmation bias (Allen & Coole, 2012; Bullough, 2014). If we are excited about a new unit and certain it is a good match for our students, we may be more likely to notice children's positive reactions and outcomes. The opposite may also happen, if our initial attempts at new content or approach go completely awry. If early lessons look different enough from the picture in our mind, then we may begin to focus only on the problems children encounter and fail to notice things that are working. Likewise, if we are upset about a new mandated curriculum that has been handed out over the summer and feel it is a step backward, we are likely to focus on evidence that supports this view unless the initial results are so different from our prediction that we toss out our initial ideas altogether.

Engaging in narrative inquiry to examine the impact of a new approach does not eliminate confirmation bias. After all, any researcher is biased in what s/he chooses to notice. Often the ways in which we elicit stories from children reflect what we want to hear, and children are keenly attuned to adults' expectations, especially those of their teacher. However, a commitment to collecting and analyzing stories of experience over time, using a variety of methods, can result in the creation of counter-narratives to the story with which we enter a new curriculum. Additionally, narrative inquiry can allow the teacher researcher to develop a richer picture of how children interact with a new curriculum and allow a finer grained analysis than our initial impression of "it's working" or "it's a failure." Narrative inquiry can also supplement and enrich the quantitative measures of success or failure that are more commonly used to measure children's progress and provide insight into *how* children make progress over time in relation to curriculum, teacher, classmates, and the classroom environment.

It is important to realize that the notion of "curriculum" looks quite different across the spectrum of early childhood and elementary classroom environments that children inhabit. At one end is the play-based, emergent curriculum common in many early childhood settings, far rarer in elementary classrooms, in which teachers may design the environment and provide materials, but the curriculum largely follows children's interests and chosen activities from day to day. At the other end are schools in which teachers are expected to teach a specific, sometimes scripted, curriculum in each subject, with little variance from classroom to classroom. In the middle, and perhaps most common in both preschool and elementary settings, is the structured but unscripted curriculum, in which teachers are required to cover set material over the course of a year, perhaps within specific timeframes, and are provided with some curricular materials, but are given professional discretion to adapt these materials based on the needs of their students. Because the emergent curriculum environment is so different in structure than the other two, we will take up separately the issue of narrative inquiry to examine curriculum in emergent environments and in structured curricular environments.

Narrative Inquiry and the Emergent Curriculum

Emergent curriculum refers most broadly to a curriculum that follows and supports children's interests, experiences, and talents. There are variations to this general framework primarily found in early childhood contexts in the U.S. (Jones & Nimmo, 1994; Jones, 2012), Canada (Wien, 2008), New Zealand (Pohio, Sansom, & Liley, 2015), and Italy (Edwards, Gandini, & Forman, 2012). In these approaches to an emergent or generative curriculum, teachers create their own instructional stories or paths that parallel and also support and guide children's individual and collective paths toward play, development, learning, and growth. Emergent curriculum frameworks often have built-in curricular flexibility and time for teachers to observe, document, and reflect on the course of student learning and teacher goals and practices. The more permeable nature of emergent work can allow for extra time and opportunities for teachers to slow down their teaching, observe student engagement and learning, and to record and document the particular story arcs and trajectories of individual and collective student learning and growth. As a result, emergent curricular approaches are often a natural fit for investigating teaching and learning through narrative inquiry methodologies. We provide a few examples of how narrative inquiry can illuminate key aspects of an emergent curriculum's potential for enhancing children's agency and voice, initiative-taking and discovery, and guided yet open-ended access to curricular content.

Gita Jayewardene (2013) embarked on a series of nature and outdoor explorations with her preschoolers in the vicinity of their San Francisco school that she documented with narrative-based observational notes, a teaching diary, and photographs. Gita grew up in Sri Lanka and loved the natural surroundings of her children, and had long been interested in pursuing more outdoor explorations with her preschoolers. Gita wanted her preschoolers living in an urban area to experience nature firsthand by seeing, touching, smelling, and hearing. She also believed in an adult-led guiding approach to emergent curriculum, having learned that children's curiosity alone is not enough to explore and learn about nature in a deep and long-lasting way. Gita and her children first explored the school's small garden area, hoping to find small animals to observe and document.

GARDEN EXPLORATION

Gita Jayewardene (2013)

I was not very hopeful that I would find enough specimens for my students to observe solely from our school play yard. But we do have many bushes with purple flowers that bloom from spring through the end of fall that attract many honeybees to the annoyance and fear of most teachers and the curiosity of the children. We also have many large trees surrounding our center but are out of reach of our children. These trees are home to many kinds of birds such as hummingbirds, bluebirds and woodpeckers and also to squirrels. I never had the chance to explore these trees and bushes around our school during the 10 years I have worked at the center. As spring was near, we started hearing different bird calls from the birds in the area, my students and I also talked about making a bird sanctuary. Then I started collecting information on how to build one. I was certain that there were also many other creatures that were making these trees and the bushes under the trees their home. I decided to get some advice on different methods of looking for different kinds of creatures from Durrell's (1988) *A Practical Guide for the Amateur Naturalist*. But until then my students and I explored under our planter boxes to see if we could find any creatures to observe. When we removed our long planter, the children were surprised to see a colony of woodlice and a slug living under it. Our nature journey had begun.

Over the next several weeks, Gita and the children explored the woodlice under the planter boxes, and then ventured out of the school to explore the trees and shrubbery in the surrounding area, and then they made weekly excursions to an environmental yard a few blocks away to study animal life, the plants, and the flowers. Gita and the children explored flowers and plants, creatures such as spiders and scorpions (in plastic cases), squirrels, ladybugs, newts, worms, woodlice, tadpoles and frogs (a firebelly toad), and birds (two parakeets); built a bird sanctuary; acted out animal actions and behaviors in their tumbling area; shared and discussed nature books; and sang nature and animal songs. During this emerging and evolving curriculum, Gita documented the children's conversations, insights, and interests, and guided the children in making closer examinations of the animals and plant life and in making representational drawings as they observed the objects and animals.

Gita could not have predicted the narrative arc of her nature journey with the children, neither predicting the children's interests and discoveries, nor the course of the curriculum content, the walks, discussions, and insights and concepts learned. These elements of "curricular surprise" befit an emergent curriculum, as the children's interests, the course of their learning processes, and our new directions and strategies as educators change and evolve as the collective experience unfolds over time, space, and understanding.

Narrative Inquiry and the Mandated Curriculum

In most elementary school settings, teachers are not entirely free to determine the curriculum based on their ongoing inquiry into students' ideas and interactions. Third-grade teachers almost always have to teach multiplication, and most schools or districts require that they use a specific set of curricular materials to do so. However, the constraints of a required curriculum do not mean that inquiry into how students respond to the curriculum is pointless. In fact, using narrative as a means to understand children's learning may provide a particularly important counterbalance to the flood of "musts" that originate outside the classroom. Consider, for example, how narrative inquiry impacts Stephanie's teaching of a science unit that is based on the Next Generation Science Standards (NGSS) for fifth grade (NGSS Lead States, 2013).

**STUDENT IDEAS VS. KNOWN FACTS
(blog entry)**

January 2015

My plan for this class was to examine the stomata on leaves and begin to discuss transpiration. I have had little success getting students to really see stomata under a microscope in the past, so I decided to try a new technique . . . putting clear nail polish on a section of the top of the leaf and also on a section of the underside. After allowing the polish to dry, students were to press packing tape into the polish-covered spot and remove the resulting impression to examine under the microscope. Planner that I am, I tried this at home with a leaf from my garden and it worked well. It was easy to see lots of stomata on the underside impression, and very few on the top.

However, in the classroom, it did not work well at all, and I'm still unsure why. Each student group was looking at a different kind of leaf, and some definitely did not take impressions as well as others. We may also not have allowed sufficient time for the nail polish to dry. And as I should have better anticipated, focusing the microscopes was difficult, despite an earlier session on microscope use, so I found myself running around troubleshooting the technology, one of my least favorite teaching roles. I hate it when groups are sitting around helpless, dependent on me to move forward.

So I found myself with ten minutes left in class and with a big dilemma on my hands. We had already gone to quite a lot of trouble in order to observe a pretty straightforward phenomena: that is, there are tiny holes all over the leaf, and there are a lot more of them on the underside than on the top side. A couple of kids in the class actually knew this already. But our observational data was not backing this up at all. In fact, the two groups that actually successfully focused their microscopes and saw anything at all were certain that there were more stomata on the tops of their leaves. At that moment, I was faced with a problem that every science teacher faces from time to time: Should I tell them what they actually should have seen and just move on, or should I stick with this now failed activity and revisit it, possibly losing a whole class period in the interest of students "discovering" a phenomena that they could also learn by reading a single sentence in any book about plants?

My in-the-moment action involved putting off that decision. I brought the class into a discussion circle and asked them to share out what they had observed, and what ideas they had about the leaf based on their observations. Never at a loss for words, most students came up with something to say. Responses included (from a student who had already displayed normative understanding): "Well, I am almost sure there are more stomata on the bottom of the leaf, but this one had more on the top, so maybe it depends on the leaf." Great, nothing like confusing kids for no reason . . . but I also got this: "I don't know what I was seeing at all! I thought the black line [the pointer on the microscope] was the most important thing, and it turns out it wasn't even part of the leaf! I think we need to get better at using the microscopes." In retrospect, I love both of these responses, because neither child was willing to draw a conclusion when it was clear they didn't have evidence to support it. That's pretty huge. Imagine a world where people didn't jump to conclusions before finding compelling evidence!

> But I left class troubled. I didn't really intend for this to be a student voice focused lesson. After all, I set up the activity and anticipated they would observe a specific, non-controversial phenomenon. Would just telling them about stomata and abandoning the investigation impact their growing science identity at all? Honestly, probably not much. And yet, I also think that every time I abandon an investigation in favor of the "right" answer, I reify the predominant idea in our society that learning science is about mastering the already known rather than searching for evidence to support or refute our ideas about the world.

In this narrative segment, in the form of a blog entry, Stephanie is working to make meaning of a puzzling class session in the middle of a science unit. In this fifth-grade class, she has specific curricular goals based on the NGSS, in this case for students to understand and describe the movement of energy and matter among plants, animals, and the environment. In order to understand how plants transform the sun's energy into energy useable for both plant growth and animal consumption, her children need to know the parts of the plant that receive and process the different "ingredients" of photosynthesis and transpiration. This is far from emergent curriculum! While the children in Stephanie's class showed great interest in the content, and as a result she chose to go deeper into the chemical processes than required at the fifth-grade level, the curriculum comes largely from adults' decisions about what science is critical to understand, not directly from the children's ideas and explorations.

This tension between the set curriculum and how children choose to take it up forms the puzzle captured in this narrative segment. If we break down the segment in terms of the simple narrative structure of story setup/problem/resolution, the segment above contains only the first two parts. She stops at the point of problem. That is, the demonstration had not given the desired results (children seeing many more stomata on the backs of the leaves than on the fronts), and the children were coming up with interesting but scientifically inaccurate explanations to describe what they had seen. Stephanie stops the narrative in the middle of the story, aware that she has the power to take the story in one of several directions. In fact, in her teaching journal, she titled a page "How will this end???" and jotted down several possible next steps, ranging from the mundane to the ridiculous. These included:

- Re-do
- Re-do with teacher assist (pre-make slides)
- Use ready-made slides of stomata (do I have front of leaf slides [for comparison]??)
- Just tell them and move on! (read page on leaf structure)
- Tell what we were "supposed" to find and discuss why we didn't
- Lie!!! Act like they saw more stomata on the underside [note this was intended as a joke!]

This approach to planning is far from revolutionary. This is the work teachers do all the time, although often in their head rather than on paper. However, because Stephanie was thinking about her students' experiences in terms of narrative, she went a step further, thinking not only about how the *lesson* would end, but how her choice of ending might impact how her *students' stories* might evolve, both in terms of their understanding of the content and in terms of their scientific identity. Her planning page ended up looking like Figure 5.1.

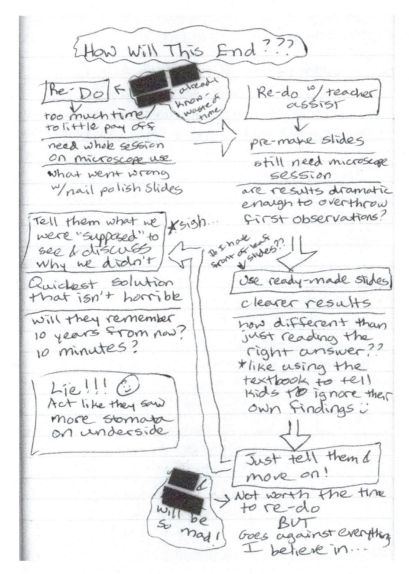

FIGURE 5.1 Planning page from Stephanie's journal.

Her ideas about how the different endings would impact specific students were, of course, conjecture. But they were conjectures based on the narratives she was collecting about how different children engaged in the science lessons and how they built understanding in relationship with the lesson content, their classmates, and Stephanie as their teacher. Consider, for instance, the note "[Tia] and [Sofia] will be mad!" (real names blacked out in Figure 5.1) A couple of weeks earlier, Stephanie had recorded a before-class conversation between her and these two students:

SOPHIA AND TIA DISCUSS SCIENCE

December 2014

Tia always checks in during recess as I'm setting up, to peek at my clipboard and figure out what we'll be doing in class. Today she had Sophia in tow. She looked over my clipboard as I blatantly pretended not to notice and continued placing bingo chips in cups. "What's a photosynthesis simulation?" she asked.

"Well, that's a great question, but as you know, I'm a mean and terrible teacher who doesn't answer her children's questions," I responded, a script we've both played our roles in many times before.

"But you HAVE to tell me. See how I'm here before class all INTERESTED and ASKING? Don't you want your students to be curious?" She played along.

"Oh, absolutely. I love them to be curious. Saves me a lot of work. I don't have to answer their questions because they're so curious, they go figure it out on their own. If my students weren't so curious, I would have to be a lot less lazy and start answering the questions, I guess."

"So mean!" Tia pretends to huff away and turns to Sophia. "She's so mean! Turning away a child who just wants to understand science."

Sophia decides to join in, adopting her drama voice. "Yeah, I've been wondering for weeks about how things decompose, and she makes me go and figure it out myself. I've got PAGES filled with notes. She could have just told me." She pauses, coming out of character, and adds in her regular voice, "Actually, I would hate that. I hate when I'm trying to figure something out and somebody just tells me. What a bunch of wasted work."

Tia responds, "Yeah, true." She turns back to me. "Okay Stephanie, [Sophia] saved you this time. But just you wait. I will get you to answer a question when you least expect it."

At the beginning of this school year, Stephanie decided to capture brief student stories after each weekly science class. As is the case with most busy teachers, she was not entirely successful in sticking with this weekly goal. However, by the time of the stomata lesson, she had a collection of 15 narratives, ranging from a paragraph to a couple of pages in length, that brought to life how students were interacting with the curriculum, with each other, and with her as a teacher. Thus, when she came to decision points in her planned curriculum, she had evidence from which she could predict students' responses to her plans. She was able to think not just about how her students would perform on an end of unit assessment, but could also focus on her goal of helping students develop their science identity. She was well aware of constraints of time, materials, and attention, and she had to balance these with her loftier goals. In this case, she made the decision to tell students what scientists generally found to be true (more stomata on the underside of the leaves, where less water will escape due to evaporation) and to have them discuss why their investigation had yielded contradictory results. She decided that the concept the investigation was meant to demonstrate was not really "worth" an entire lesson re-do. However, her examination of collected student narratives made her attuned to the reactions that came up during the class discussion.

STUDENTS DISCUSS STOMATA: ROUND 2

January 2015

"Well that was a waste of time!" Tyler's reaction was met with a couple of subtle nods before Amara held out her hands for the koosh ball [the class' way of monitoring conversations]. In her quiet voice, she said, "I think we didn't make the slides very well. When I was looking in the microscope, I wasn't really sure if I was counting stomata or something else. If a scientist was doing this, they would know what they were seeing. It wouldn't be so confusing."

She tossed the ball to Ali, who said, "But what if we were the first scientists seeing it? I mean, the first scientist wouldn't know that they weren't seeing the stomata, because, um . . . " he trailed off, as he often does, not sure how to explain his thought. Gabriel put out his hands, moving to fill in words for his friend. Ali hesitated and then passed the ball.

"Yeah, they wouldn't know they were supposed to see a bunch of holes in the leaf, or they wouldn't know why they were there. We only know we got it wrong because we weren't the first ones to figure it out."

Tyler wasn't convinced and waved for the ball. He said, "But maybe we were right. Maybe some leaves have more stomata on top [of the leaf]. It may not *always* be true that there are more on the bottom. Like maybe in a wet place it wouldn't matter about the evaporation so they'd be all over the leaf."

Sophia jumped in: "But there aren't really rainforest plants on the yard [of the school, where students picked the leaves]. I'm pretty sure we just did it wrong. It does make sense that the stomata would be on the bottom."

This brief analysis of a single lesson did not radically shift the content or sequence of Stephanie's curriculum. However, it did cause her to rethink the purpose and impact of hands on investigations that were intended to demonstrate a known fact rather than encourage problem solving and exploration. The "what a waste of time" response from Tyler revealed a frustration that Stephanie shared with some of her students, that there was not much joy (and probably little long-term retention) of projects in which the results would be discarded if they did not go as expected. As a result of her analysis of this segment of the curriculum, she decided to begin her unit the following year with a more open-ended exploration of leaves, and to use the questions generated as a way to provide "just in time" factual information as needed.

Narrative inquiry often allows for this type of subtle, ongoing analysis of curriculum through understanding children's learning in terms of their stories. However, sometimes this type of inquiry causes teachers to question the utility of their curriculum at a more fundamental level. Nicole Ginocchio, a second-grade teacher in Oakland, California, began to collect stories of her students' experiences with the mandated and highly scripted literacy curriculum in use at her school. Her impression before her inquiry began was that the children, most of whom were English Learners simultaneously learning to read and learning to speak and understand English, really disliked literacy instruction. In collecting stories of their experiences, she found that what they most disliked was a section of each day called "fluency" in which they were to repeatedly read assigned, leveled texts in order to develop fluent oral reading. It appeared from the children's descriptions of their experiences that they felt no autonomy during this activity, and this often showed up in the form of disengagement and misbehavior. Ginocchio's first step, inviting her students to share their opinions and to criticize the curriculum as implemented, was a move toward not only analyzing her practice but also toward changing the story of her students' experiences and feelings of power in the classroom.

Despite the strong mandate from her school that she follow the curriculum as written, Ginocchio began to experiment with small changes to the fluency block each day. First, although she continued to use the required "decodable," leveled texts, she placed out several of them each day and let reading groups choose what to read. This change that increased children's degree of choice during a mandated activity had a slight but noticeable positive effect. She then worked with a single small group to test out other ideas for increasing enjoyment of fluency practice. This group had been particularly vocal about wanting more choice in their reading, and so she was curious if honoring their request would work to increase interest and enjoyment. First, they moved from the required decodable text to more story-rich selections from the second grade reading anthology. Ginocchio recorded a marked increase in students' enjoyment as this change was implemented. Then, in response to the group's interest, she introduced readers' theater, another well-tested method for increasing fluency, which the group worked on during fluency time in lieu of the mandated texts. During the readers' theater sessions, every student in the focus group reported enjoying their fluency practice.

By seeking out the narratives of her students' experiences with the mandated curriculum, Ginocchio came to question her role as "enforcer" of a set of activities that the children disliked and that did not seem to benefit them. She allowed her students to alter the story of the classroom, serving as critics, not simply as receptacles for the literacy curriculum's intended goals. Given what she learned from her students, she was compelled to make changes to the curriculum that kept intact the instructional goals (in this case more fluent reading of grade level texts) but that also honored her students' lived experiences. She was somewhat nervous about veering from the strictly enforced mandates of the school's adopted curriculum, but she felt the stories of her students required that she honor them.

Children as Co-Inquirers

Children's lived stories of classroom life are at the heart of teachers' narrative inquiry. In order to understand the impact of curricular choices, teachers must elicit their students' experiences and use the stories that emerge as the basis for instructional decisions. Sometimes, however, students can play an even more active role in curricular inquiry, engaging in their own analysis of their and others' stories as a way of improving learning and teaching in their classrooms.

Ginocchio's experience with making changes to her literacy fluency block shows that inviting children to tell their stories and the engage in criticism can make them active proponents of changing what is not working for them. In addition, opening up instructional inquiry to children can make them aware of their own power to change the story in progress. Several regular practices can support the development of students as co-inquirers.

Broaden the Search for Stories Beyond the School Walls

In Herbert Kohl's classic book, *The Discipline of Hope*, this lifelong educator captures the stories of many of his students from a wide variety of settings over a 40-year teaching career. In the opening chapter, he writes of his first year as a teacher in New York City, struggling to reconcile his plan to teach an interactive but non-controversial version of a Eurocentric curriculum with the disconnect and outright defiance he feels from his students. As an outsider to the community in terms of background, race, and socioeconomic status, he decided that he needed to understand the worlds of his students before he could make decisions about how to teach them. He began by asking them to write about the blocks on which they lived. The descriptions that poured in of poverty and crime, and also of pride and community, helped him get to know his students, but did little to help him connect the curriculum to his children's lives. He continued to ask them to write about their lives, though, and he found them eager to do so. They wrote not only about their worlds as they were, but also about what they would choose to change. As he continued to invite and analyze these stories, he decided to introduce the study of ancient civilizations as a means to investigate "the creation of society and the potential for people to live in groups governed by compassion and mutual aid" (Kohl, 1998, p. 33). Through seeking to understand the lived and imagined stories of his students, he found his way into the curriculum in a way that held meaning and interest for the particular group of children he was charged with teaching.

Sometimes we think of asking children about their lives outside of school as a necessary beginning of the year task, a way to get to know students before charging ahead with the work we must do. But when we place children's stories at the forefront of our work, the way that we and they interact with the curriculum necessarily changes. Taking time to regularly elicit stories of children's lives beyond school helps us build ongoing connections between the material we are to teach and the ways in which children may find meaning.

Frame Reflections in Narrative Terms

"Tell me a story" is a prompt with a fundamentally different feel than "tell me what you learned." Prompting children to reflect through the use of narrative helps teachers to identify what is most important and meaningful to children. Vivian Gussin Paley's work with young children highlights the ways in which engaging children in storytelling allows teachers to build understanding and make instructional decisions. In *The Boy Who Would Be a Helicopter* (1990), Paley explores the impact of her classroom's storytelling culture on a boy, Jason, who generally secludes himself from the activities of others. In Paley's classroom, she invites children to dictate stories to her and to act them out, and she uses her role as teacher to remind children of the stories they tell her and to use them as windows into recurring ideas and struggles. Paley writes:

> Amazingly, children are born knowing how to put every thought and feeling into story form. If they worry about being lost, they become the parents who search; if angry, they find a hot hippopotamus to impose his will upon the world. Even happiness has its plot and characters: "Pretend I'm the baby and you only love me and you don't talk on the telephone." (p. 4)

In her account, she examines Jason as a child who remains largely outside the ever evolving stories in her preschool class. She writes: "He speaks only of helicopters and broken blades, and he appears indifferent to the play and stories that surround him." (p. 11). As Paley seeks to understand this child who does not fit her existing theory of how young children relate to one another through story, the other children continually make moves to include Jason and his helicopter in their stories. Jason does not outwardly respond, continuing to focus, day after day, on fixing the broken blades of his imagined helicopter. Despite Paley's puzzlement at this child who does not want to join in the stories of others, she notices that to the other children, Jason seems to make sense. She continues to observe and record the stories in which children work to include Jason, even when he does not respond. And as she continues to pay attention, she sees signs that Jason is, in fact, engaging with others. When another child, Simon, is performing his story on the tape bounded "stage" in the classroom, and Jason interrupts by flying his helicopter through, Simon includes him in the story and tells him where to land, and he does. Jason follows this by telling his own story on the stage for the first time, including Simon in his helicopter story.

By focusing on children's stories, and by envisioning her work as a recorder and encourager of stories, Paley begins to see not only Jason's outsider status, but also the places of inclusion that children make for him and how these small, repeated interactions show his importance to their community. If Paley had focused her observations on more discrete skill learning, she might have only ever seen the ways in which Jason did not fit among more typically developing peers. But in focusing on narrative, both the children's imaginative story and her own emerging story in relation to the children, she found points of entry and ways that Jason contributed to and made stronger the stories of this class.

Beyond the preschool years, the power of storytelling and narrative structure as a way to make meaning is sometimes lost in the race to master "academic" language and texts. And yet our brain's wiring for story does not end with the commencement of schooling. Children and adults alike attend to narrative more than to other forms of information delivery. This may be because stories are inherently interesting and because attending to story requires our brains to make continual, small inferences, thus actively involving us in a way that other forms of reporting do not (Willingham, 2004). When we hear stories, our brains automatically seek causal connections, even where none are provided. This natural inclination of our brains can be tremendously useful to teachers trying to investigate how children are responding to curriculum. Consider, for instance, this reflection from Kevin, a third grader who was prompted to "tell the story" of a case of natural selection the class had studied (Kevin is telling this story orally to a student from another class as part of a cross-class activity).

KEVIN'S STORY OF THE CRICKETS ON KAUAI

There was once, there's this scientist that went to this island called Kauai and there's these crickets. There's these chirping male crickets and some non-chirping male crickets. So the scientist saw that the chirping crickets had the survival advantage. So the [chirpers] had the survival advantage, so the so the chirping crickets reproduced, they mated. To the next generation. Then the fly came. This kind of fly laid eggs in crickets and um, in the crickets so that hurt mostly the chirping crickets. So now the non-chirping crickets have the survival advantage and fifteen generations later the scientist came back and there were a few chirping crickets and mostly non-chirping crickets.

When Stephanie listened to Kevin tell this story, her first response was that he had really understood the ideas of natural selection well. Kevin's response had enough "markers" from the narrative as discussed in class that Stephanie's brain was able to fill in the details, thus assuming that he fully understood. When she listened to it again, though, she made a list of causal links that were missing ("answers" are in brackets to make the phenomenon clear to the reader)

- Why did the chirping crickets have a survival advantage at the beginning of the story? [They used chirping to find a mate, so chirpers are more likely to mate and have offspring.]
- Why did the fly laying its eggs hurt mostly the chirping crickets? [The fly found crickets to lay eggs in by listening for the chirping, so chirpers were most often victims.]
- Why did the non-chirpers gain a survival advantage? [They were less likely to be caught by the fly.]
- Why aren't the chirping crickets extinct? [They still have a mating advantage.]

It is possible, of course, that Kevin understood all of the causal links and merely omitted them in his retelling of the story. However, by listening carefully, and repeatedly, to Kevin's narrative, Stephanie saw potential gaps in understanding that might not have been clear in a more traditional assessment. In her role as teacher and researcher, this insight alone might be enough justification for such an activity as part of her regular classroom practice. But even more compelling was the opportunity to bring her students into the process of seeking connections through narrative.

Kevin told his version of cricket evolution to a partner from another class who had studied the same science concept (natural selection) in a different domain (aster seeds rather than crickets). After cross-class pairs shared their stories, Stephanie and her partner teacher from the other class convened cross-class discussions in which they asked students to identify similarities in the two narratives of natural selection. The students readily identified a number of similarities between the stories, similarities that exist in any case of natural selection: the survival value of certain traits over others, the existence of environmental pressure, the more likely passing on of the advantageous trait due to increased survival of organisms with this trait. However, in their discussion, they also identified ideas that they did not fully understand. In the group Stephanie facilitated, students from the botany class realized that they had not identified what the environment of their plants was like *before* the environmental change. In the cricket example, there was a clear advantage for chirping crickets until the predator fly arrived, and then a clear advantage for non-chirping crickets. For the botany group, who studied a case of heavier and lighter seeds after they landed on an island, they realized they did not know the beginning of the story, before the seeds got to the island.

By inviting children to think of their content in narrative terms and then asking them to listen to others' narratives and compare them, the children entered into the process of analyzing their own understanding. In so doing, they identified a part of the curriculum that was missing, yet had been invisible to their teachers. This process allowed them to reflect on their own interaction with the curriculum as presented as well as to serve as tellers and retellers of stories that are core to the understanding of science.

Invite Critique

When Nicole Ginocchio began her inquiry into her students' feelings of ownership and motivation, she committed a brave act at the outset that impacted the rest of her study. She invited her students to critique the literacy curriculum, to tell her what was not working and what they wished was different. Inviting critique is difficult for most people. Asking others to tell us what we are not doing well can leave us feeling vulnerable and unsure. Teachers spend countless hours planning and implementing lessons with the hope that they will inspire and motivate their students. Asking these students if the lessons worked as intended opens up the possibility that the children will reveal our failure.

In Ginocchio's case, she was well aware that most of her students disliked the literacy block. Their dislike puzzled her in part because she herself had loved school as a child, and so she was unprepared to encounter a classroom of children who had learned to dislike school so early in their lives. Rather than shifting blame and assuming something was wrong with the children in her class, she was certain that something must be wrong with the learning environment to make them so resistant. And perhaps more remarkably, she was not willing to abdicate her responsibility to address the issue even though, at the time, her school district mandated that she use specific instructional materials for specified time periods and in a required sequence. Despite the system-imposed restrictions, Ginocchio thought that she, with her students' help, could create a more positive, motivating learning environment. And so as she collected her students' stories, she repeatedly asked them to evaluate how lessons had gone, what they liked, and what could have been better. In doing so, she directly involved her students in investigating the problem of motivation during learning. She did not just gather their stories for her own analysis. Rather, she asked them to consider the emerging stories of their own and their classmates' experience with the curriculum and to offer feedback that impacted future lessons.

While inviting critique can feel risky if it has not been done before, creating a structure for it as a regular part of classroom practice is not difficult. Older children can complete a short reflection at the end of each lesson in a particular subject, or at the end of each week. A simple format might look like Figure 5.2.

		Math Reflection		
How much I learned today				
1	2	3	4	5
How much I enjoyed today				
1	2	3	4	5
What went well?				
What do you hope is different next time?				

FIGURE 5.2   Math reflection.

Alternately, an end of class or end of day ritual might involve gathering the children in a circle and asking them to respond to a few reflective prompts such as:

- The best part of today was . . .
- Something I learned was . . .
- If I could change one thing I would . . .
- Tomorrow I hope . . .

Sometimes teachers can quite directly ask students to tell them what worked and did not work during a lesson or a school day. However, children are very kind, and often they are quite hesitant to say something that they believe would hurt the teacher's feelings. Developing routines that invite critique helps by providing a safe space and sending a message that critique is part of the culture of the class, not a way of insulting the teacher's best efforts.

Ask Children to Help Change the Story

In Herbert Kohl's account of his first year teaching, he describes his feeling of helplessness when he first invited his students to write about their blocks and saw the huge disconnect between their lives and the curriculum he was supposed to teach. As he realized the importance of understanding his children's lives in and out of school, though, he continued to elicit their experiences and ideas. He asked them to write about what they would change about their blocks if they could change anything. The animated responses led to a study of ancient civilizations focused on understanding how societies develop and how they can change. By prioritizing the children's lived experiences in and out of school, he conveyed the message that they had power to impact what went on within school walls.

When teachers feel that the curriculum is not going well or is failing to connect with children, inviting them to participate in changing it for the better can improve not only learning but also children's connection to school and to the community of classmates and teachers. When Stephanie taught fifth grade in a classroom in which there were uneven and often belligerent patterns of participation that left many children scared to speak up, she decided to directly point out her observations to the class. She asked for their ideas to help address the problems that they were experiencing. Although hesitant to contribute ideas at first, the students ended up developing a number of novel strategies that increased everyone's awareness of participation and classroom norms. LoAnn, a very quiet child in the class, suggested that there be an observer in each class who made tally marks to note who participated. While this felt a bit unsafe to Stephanie, the class was wildly in favor of the idea. Stephanie suggested that the tally charts be submitted to her, and she would compile the data without names. Over a period of a few weeks, it became clear to the students that boys completely dominated most class conversations. They suggested single-gender table groups, another idea that Stephanie hated, but which the children embraced enthusiastically. And in fact, in single-gendered groups the girls spoke up and reported much higher engagement. The children on their own came to the conclusion that the groups should not always be separate. One girl, Nai, who was gregarious among girls but more reluctant in the whole group setting, said, "I think being with just girls makes me braver. Then when I'm in a group with boys I know I have something to say and maybe I'll say it more 'cause I'm not as scared."

Feelings of belonging and autonomy are a basic human need. When we invite children into the process of not just telling their stories but also changing stories for the better, we help them feel power over their own lives and responsibility for shaping a better world for themselves and for those around them. And when we allow children's voices to impact what and how we teach, schools become living, changing environments that support both teachers and students to be fully engaged in the story of schools.

6

NARRATIVE INQUIRY AND LANGUAGE AND LITERACY TEACHING

Narrative inquiry can deepen and widen our understanding of how we conceptualize our language and literacy philosophies, curriculum, and instructional practices, and do so within the cultural traditions and talents of educators, students, and families. As discussed in this chapter, there are several key elements for successfully incorporating narrative inquiry into language and literacy teaching.

Social and Cultural Identities

Narrative inquiry is an approach intimately linked to the ways that children and adults use languages and literacies inside and outside educational settings. How we think, move, feel, and think as human beings is largely dependent upon our internal and external languages, which are influenced to a great extent by our social and cultural traditions and talents. The forms and functions of the languages that adults and children use in educational settings are closely linked with the languages that we depend on for daily discourse, social communication and bonding, intellectual understanding, and affirmation of our identities as individuals and as members of multiple communities. In educational contexts, narrative inquiry has the potential to give voice to English language learners' often hidden talents and needs (Hong & Genishi, 2005; Souto-Manning, 2007), link funds of knowledge to the curriculum (Quintero, 2015), highlight African-American children's talents for code-meshing multiple languages and literacies (Young, Barrett, Young-Rivera, & Lovejoy, 2014), and illuminate the perspectives and experiences of young emergent bilinguals and their families (García & Kleifgen, 2010).

A Playful Orientation Toward Language

As an approach that values experimentation and puzzle-making, narrative inquiry also shares an affinity with a playful stance toward language and literacy instruction. The idea of narrative inquiry as a puzzle, as a journey of some unknowns and even magic and mystery, fits well with an approach to language and literacy education that values the unpredictable in conversations and discussions. For the consummate early childhood teacher Vivian Paley, story is an essential glue for integrating play and children's language learning (Cooper, 2011; Gadzikowski, 2007; McNamee, 2005; Paley, 1981). A philosophical and curricular devotion to the power of story makes us better listeners of children's ideas and languages, better observers and interpreters of their literacy products, and helps form social and intellectual bonds in the classroom. Paley's devotion to story as the center of her teaching creates "common ground in the classroom where the minds of children and teacher meet and grow over the course of a school year" (McNamee, 2005, p. 277).

Children's Language and Literacy Development

Narrative inquiry helps us observe, document, and analyze looking at aspects of children's language and literacy engagement over time (McNamee, 2005; Meier, 2000; Paley, 1990). If we employ selected narrative inquiry tools from our Chapter 3, we can examine the language and literacy development of an individual child, a small group of children, or the whole class, grade level, or even school. We can "slice" the teaching and learning data we collect to examine a single, critical narrative point in the children's learning—for instance, looking at all of the children's engagement within a single dictation or writing activity. Or, we can look at a few or several narrative points, such as the beginning, middle, and end of the children's engagement with a writing project or set of activities over a few days, weeks, or even months. This allows us to look both at what might change and what might remain constant over a long period of time, in effect stretching the narrative arc for children's learning as well as our own teaching, providing more developmental breadth and depth for our reflection and analysis. And in a world of rapidly changing technologies and communication expectations, we will continue to see new forms and functions for language and literacy (Ferreiro, 2003), altering the characters and settings and plot lines for children's literacy, as well as what we now recognize as expected developmental arcs for children's language and literacy development.

Language and Literacy Education—Philosophy and Instruction

Narrative inquiry allows us to look at the professional trajectory of our language and literacy instruction over our teaching years and experiences (Ballenger, 1999; Meier, 1997; Paley, 1981). For novice teachers, this might mean looking in the here and now at what is going well, what is not, and the hoped-for next steps to increase our competency for language and literacy teaching. For educators in this more novel position, the narrative arc of one's teaching preparation and effectiveness often parallels the arc of the students' language and literacy engagement and learning. More veteran teachers might employ narrative inquiry for looking back on one's language and literacy teaching, as well current teaching, and also looking ahead; the gift of experience affords us a longer continuum of language and literacy moments, vignettes, and stories for refining one's teaching philosophy and collection of effective instructional strategies.

Professional Growth and Knowledge

Narrative inquiry also supports our understanding of a particular language and literacy curricular or teaching idea or theory or strategy over time (Goswami & Rutherford, 2009; Phillips & Gallas, 2004; Souto-Manning, 2006). For instance, this might involve examining strategies for whole-class read-alouds, and tracking which strategies we adapt and improve over time, and documenting children's responses, ideas, and language during the read-alouds. Or we might look at the trajectory, or journey, of student engagement with writing long stories on the computer over the course of a month. For instance, as discussed later in this chapter, the National Novel Writing Month, or NaNoWriMo (http://ywp .nanowrimo.org/), offers students a chance to write their own novels over the course of November each year. If students have not had the opportunity to write and track their writing (length, grammar, content, characters, plot development, etc.) over an entire month, this can be another example of a new instructional strategy and routine for examining its effects on student writing development.

Taken together, the four narrative inquiry themes discussed above promote a disposition and inquisitive stance toward language and literacy teaching and learning. In a central way, they contribute to an "intellectual tradition" in which we "examine and explicitly articulate the relationship between others' work and our own, and to understand the influence that work has on our practice" (Goswami & Rutherford, 2009, p. 8). The work of "others" can include our closest teaching colleagues, colleagues at other institutions, as well as the work of researchers and policymakers in the area of language and literacy education. In this sense, the particular narrative inquiry points of our practice and reflection spread out, touching the perspectives and inquiry of colleagues and other educators, thus widening the "narrative net" of our teaching and deepening our professional growth and knowledge.

Narrative Inquirers Explore Language and Literacy Education

This section describes and discusses extended examples of narrative inquiry in preschool, transitional kindergarten, and fifth grade and examines key elements of children's language and literacy learning. The discussion also highlights the role of the inquiry projects not only for understanding children's language and literacy growth, but for deepening narrative inquirers' professional growth and knowledge.

Read-Alouds and Personal Journals—Preschool

In Daniel's work in a public preschool classroom in the San Francisco East Bay, he conducted a whole-group read-aloud and small-group work with children drawing and dictating in their personal journals. Each week, as Daniel took notes on his hour-long literacy session in the classroom, Daniel looked for evidence of changes in the levels of children's language and literacy engagement and interest in the activities, and also the degree to which the children incorporated elements of the read-alouds in their personal journals. As he taught, Daniel also observed and took notes both during and after the children worked in their journals. After five months, Daniel finally began to see new benefits of the whole-class read-aloud and the small-group journal session he had refined since September. He began to have more success in extending the children's level of engagement in the read-alouds, and adapting the routine to promote such "skills" as recognizing initial sounds, rhyming, vocabulary knowledge, sequencing, and plot predictions. In the small-group work, Daniel learned not to push the connections between the read-aloud books and the children's too explicitly, but rather to improve the selection of the books that the children could relate to and could adapt in their drawing and dictation. By January, then, Daniel had reached a critical narrative juncture in his time in the classroom, both for his understanding of the particular children's language and literacy development, and his understanding of more effective instructional strategies.

WHOLE GROUP READ-ALOUD

January 7, 2016

Daniel

We started by rereading several of Nina Crews' *Neighborhood Mother Goose* rhymes that I had enlarged at a Xerox store on to single large sheets, which I donated to the classroom. More of the children are remembering the rhymes, and more are predicting rhyming words. We also reread *Dinner at the Panda Palace*, and now more children are identifying the animals and remembering the number of animals who enter on each page. For new books, we read *What a Tale* and also *Whose Shoes*, both by Brian Wildsmith, and they very much enjoyed both, guessing the name of the shoes in *Shoes* and matching the tails in *What a Tale* with the corresponding animals shown at the end. *What a Tale* proved popular with a few children during the journal session later, see below.

During the read-aloud session on that day, Daniel slowed down and paused his reading of both the familiar and unfamiliar texts, because he now knew the children better, and recognized which aspects of the read-alouds were most effective. In essence, Daniel saw more effective ways to orchestrate and adapt these elements:

- the particular books chosen for the read-aloud
- the order of reading these particular books
- how many times to reread and revisit certain books
- a healthy ratio of familiar and unfamiliar books
- refining the body movements children contribute in synchrony with the text and illustration
- increasing pausing so children could contribute a missing rhyming or content word
- increasing brief explanations of vocabulary definitions or synonyms
- increasing brief connections between books by the same author, and similar genre and/or content

For instance, Daniel remembered in choosing the books for the read-aloud that the children had loved the first of Brian Wildsmith's small books that feature spare text and engaging visuals. So Daniel returned to the Wildsmith's books and selected two new ones for the read-aloud. Daniel reminded the children that they had already read some of Wildsmith's books (*The Apple Bird* and *The Island*), and that here were two new ones. In *Whose Shoes*, the children laughed as Daniel asked, "What is this shoe?" and they tried to identify the shoe on each page—ice skates, sneakers, clown shoes, roller skates (no one recognized these), rain boots, ballet slippers, "fancy party shoes," and then on the last page an animal that the children called a "caterpillar" wearing all the shoes plus others. In *What a Tale*, the first few pages describe the tails depicted—"Spotted tail" and then "Spotted tail, striped tail"—the second-to-last page shows the faces of the animals that the tails belong to in order—"Dog, cat, fox, rabbit, monkey"—and the very last page shows the animals inside the pouch of a kangaroo with the line, "What a tale." The children were delighted with both books' text and visuals, and the physical transformation of the shoes onto the caterpillar and the tails to the animals in the kangaroo's pouch. Daniel was surprised at the degree to which the children were taken with Wildsmith's two small books, and their delight reminded Daniel that the plot points of his teaching narrative needed to remain adaptable to the plot points of the children's learning narratives.

> Story is one of the most powerful cognitive tools students have available for imaginatively engaging with knowledge. Stories shape our emotional understanding of their content. Stories can share real-world content as well

as fictional material. It is this real-world story-shaping that promises most value for teaching. (Egan, 2005, p. 2)

Over Daniel's first several visits to the classroom, he had searched for more effective ways for the children to successfully integrate the whole-group read-alouds with the small-group work in their journals. It had become a "narrative sticking point" in the arc of Daniel's teaching that was building in tension, and needed some measure of resolution. On the early January session, without the aid of the book, Carolina took a red colored pencil and a half-circle and five objects on top to represent the tails in *What a Tale*, and as she pointed to each tail, Carolina dictated to Daniel as he wrote down her words above where she pointed, "This is the dog." "This is the cat." "The fox." "Bunny." "Monkey." Twenty minutes later, Trina finished her drawing, a carefully rendered representation of the animals' tails in brown marker. As she pointed to each tail, she also dictated, "This is the spotted tail." "This is the striped tail." "That's the bushy tail." "The long tail."

Daniel realized that Trina, like Carolina, had also not referred to the book for her drawing (Daniel had placed the books out for this very purpose, thinking it would amplify the links to the read-aloud and serve as a drawing model). Daniel thought at this point it might help for identifying the animals, and so Daniel and Trina opened to the page in the book depicting the animals. Trina dictated as she pointed, "Dog," "Cat," "Fox," "Monkey," and Daniel wrote down each animal in parentheses after Trinity's initial tale dictation.

In his journal, Brandon drew wavy, non-representational lines in blue and red, and then two small figures at the top of the page. Brandon dictated, "A bear." Daniel realized that he was referring to the copy of *Bear and Hare Go Fishing* beside him, but Daniel didn't see him opening the book and look at it. Daniel then picked up the book and asked Brandon which part he wanted to dictate about. "The big ol' fish." Daniel turned to the page showing the large yellowish-gold fish that Bear finally catches. Daniel restarted Brandon's dictation, hoping he'd extend it, "A bear and a hare go fishing, and at the end . . . " To which Brandon then added, "He catches a big ol' fish."

Carolina, Trina, and Brandon all used the read-aloud books as the basis for their journal drawing and dictation. Carolina and Trina referred to a book from that day's read-aloud, and Brandon had referred to a book that Daniel had read three or four times prior, but not more recently than two weeks ago. None of the children had actually looked at the books on the table as they drew, and only looked at the books' illustrations when Daniel picked up the books and opened to a particular page. Daniel's initial goal, dating back to September, of having the children link the read-alouds with their journals finally began working at a deeper and more organic level with Carolina, Trina, and Brandon. Daniel was surprised that it worked so well with three children for whom it was their very first day with the small-group journal work. The beginning of the children's learning trajectory meshed nicely with the mid-point of Daniel's teaching trajectory, creating a happy confluence of his teaching goals and strategies and the children's expanding understanding of social, cognitive, linguistic, and artistic connections across texts in multiple contexts.

Promoting Multilingualism for Children and Adults—Preschool

Narrative inquiry can be an effective approach for administrators to promote and document teachers' professional growth and development in the area of language and literacy education. Rachel Castro worked as a site supervisor of a federally funded Head Start preschool in the San Francisco Bay area serving primarily Spanish-speaking Latina/o children and their families. In an inquiry project (Castro, 2015), Rachel collaborated with three teachers in one classroom whose language skills in Spanish were stronger than their English proficiency. Rachel, a Spanish/English bilingual educator, is deeply committed to preserving and honoring the home languages of the children, the families, and the teachers. Rachel was initially interested in helping one English-speaking child improve his engagement at morning circle time, and thought that the introduction of English at this important classroom routine would help support this child's learning. As a veteran educator, Rachel also remembered another child a few years earlier, also an English-only speaker who felt comfortable and successful at circle time because Rachel had conducted her circle time activities in English.

Since Rachel could not lead circle time on a regular basis, Rachel thought of creative ways that the teachers could introduce read-alouds to add some measure of English language and literacy during the circle time activities. Rachel also remembered that last year, when she taught at another Head Start center, she had implemented shared reading of poetry based on the theme for the month in her classroom. So Rachel went back to visit her old school to observe how the teachers were organizing the shared poetry reading, and to see which elements Rachel might adapt and use at her new school with her colleagues.

Choosing three poems ("Itsy Bitsy Spider/*La Arana Peqenita*," "Here is the Beehive," and "Snowflakes, Snowflakes") for their engaging rhythm and rhyme and translations in Spanish, Rachel spoke with her colleagues about how they might start the project. It was decided that Rachel would start by modeling a shared reading of the "Itsy Bitsy Spider" in English in the classroom over two days, and then hand it over to the teachers for the rest of the week. One of the teachers with the least amount of English proficiency continued reading the poem for a second, additional week, as Rachel thought that this poem was the easiest to read in English of the three poems.

After a few weeks, Rachel noticed that the children were using more English phrases, and so Rachel discussed with the teachers new ways to extend the Spanish-speaking children's English language development. Rachel and the teachers also discussed new strategies to promote more Spanish-language learning for the several primarily English-speaking children in the classroom.

Rachel and the teachers decided to divide the children into small groups for discussion during the established shared poetry time, selecting groups of primarily Spanish-speaking children in groups with whom the teachers would mostly speak in English, and then groups for the primarily English-speaking children who would receive teacher talk mostly in Spanish. Rachel and the teachers continued to use the poems and also added visuals of the poems to further enhance the exchange of oral language in Spanish and English. Rachel wanted the sessions to be supportive, so that if children began speaking in a language that was not their designated group language, Rachel and the teachers did not correct a child, but simply repeated the phrase back to the child in the designated group language.

Rachel and her colleagues also began to see new evidence of code-switching of English and Spanish, and certain children acquired new vocabulary and phrases in a second language that helped them navigate social relationships in the classroom. While the implementation of the shared poetry and the language-specific small groups did not entirely strengthen the circle time engagement of the one particular child, which was Rachel's original motivation, the new process did make important whole-class improvements to the teachers' and children's use of Spanish and English for social and academic purposes. In terms of next steps, Rachel and her team were interested in using these newly constructed language-specific small groups during other times of the classroom day.

Rachel and the teachers were initially confronted with a teaching and learning puzzle—how to help support the one child during morning circle time. Then, relying on her teaching memories as a veteran educator, Rachel remembered another child at a previous school, a new child from Mexico, who had benefitted from home language support to transition into the classroom. Rachel's idea, though, for a new plotline of instruction in the classroom (more English at circle time) was complicated by the teachers' relative language strengths in Spanish. Then, again relying on her memory of successful strategies, Rachel returned to her previous Head Start school and looked at how her former colleagues were using a shared poetry reading routine. Rachel then created a shared, collaborative process with her current teachers to implement shared poetry reading as well as language-designated small groups with the children. The narrative arc of the instructional changes not only benefited the children's Spanish and English use, but also promoted the teachers' professional growth and knowledge of curricular adaptations in the areas of early literacy and multilingualism.

Young Children's Multilingualism and Early Literacy—Transitional Kindergarten

Narrative inquiry can also help us observe, document, and reflect on the often hard-to-see intersections between young children's multilingualism, drawing, dictation, and early writing. Sophia Jimenez (2015), who has taught transitional kindergarten (TK) for three years at a public elementary school in the San Francisco South Bay, was interested in understanding how drawing and writing contributed to her students' sense of themselves as competent individuals and students. As transitional kindergarten is a key developmental stage for bridging preschool and the new literacy demands of kindergarten, and there was no official TK curriculum and standards, Sophia wanted to find developmentally appropriate and effective ways to support her students' writing and also improve their social skills. Sophia was especially interested in understanding writing as a way "to explore aspects of their lives that excite, perplex, interest, scare, and excite them." Sophia collected her students' drawing and writing over the course of several weeks in the fall, and also documented the children's conversations and interactions through photographs and audiotaped recordings. Sophia's inquiry helped her discover a few key dimensions of her students' writing, which reinforced Sophia's knowledge of key connections between multilingualism, drawing, dictation, and early writing at the transitional kindergarten level.

First, she looked at how much drawing and writing enabled her students to spread their wings in terms of their oral language and their enjoyment of early writing. Gael drew three quite expressive pictures in purple marker and wrote accompanying text to create his "Battle of Zip" story. Sophia then asked Gael to tell his story, which Sophia recorded on an iPad.

> Page 1: It's the battle of Z-I-P. Zip. That's the VIPs, Zips. That means we are going to battle no one. The yellow teams going to be Dark Vader and the purple team going to be my team. And on my team they have all the technology.
> Page 2: And right here is like where everyone was liking him. That's . . . and then
> Page 3: This one right here is like when we were just lasering. This is Clyde. This is me. That's me. Someone's cell right there and that's was Rod with the triangle shirt. And then Emit pumped up the gas, and then I use a cannon and this is called the Dark.

Sophia noticed that the opportunity to choose his own writing topic helped Gael become engaged with his story, and to begin to enjoy drawing and writing.

Sophia's inquiry project also provided her with an opportunity to differentiate her writing instruction. She experimented with providing her English learners with story starters and sentence frames to support their writing and their emerging knowledge of English syntactical structures. For instance, in response to a class field trip to a local farm, Ana wrote an animal story based on the prompt, "I saw a _____."

> Page 1 Farm
> Page 2 I saw a goat.
> Page 3 I saw a cow.
> Page 4 I saw a goat.

When Ana read back her writing, Sophia realized that it was the first time that Ana felt like a writer, having written more than she had since the beginning of school. And at the day's end, Ana was the first volunteer to read her writing in front of the class.

Sophia also discovered that early writing also promotes content knowledge, a critical element of her school's transitional kindergarten program as preparation for kindergarten. In particular, her students' writing helped them engage with her classroom's content themes. Cristian, also an English learner, drew a picture of a flower growing above and below ground, and one cloud with rain drops coming down and another cloud with drops going in. The class had studied plant growth and water evaporation, and Cristian's drawing indicates his content knowledge in this area. Instead of asking Cristian to write, and not wanting to pressure him to speak in English, Sophia encouraged Cristian to dictate in Spanish, and his (translated) dictated text was: "dust (he meant food), flower, roots" and "water" needed for the flower's growth.

In a third discovery, Sophia collected data on her children's first attempts at conventional sound-symbol correspondence in their writing. Cora, one student, wrote three rows of letters and then three human figures below. Although she did not track the letters from left to right, Cora did read back her writing to Sophia as if it were a "real" message and written conventionally. Cora reread it to Sophia a few times, and although each rereading differed slightly, her "story" remained on the same topic, about playing with three of her friends. Maria, another child, drew a picture of a house and wrote, "MI HOUS," and Sophia noticed that Maria stretched out each sound in the words just as Sophia models in their whole-class interactive writing sessions. This brief text marked Maria's most extensive attempt at conventional spelling.

The inquiry project allowed Sophia to observe and document a series of "moments in time" of her students' early writing efforts. She discovered that her students had talent and eagerness, previously hidden, for linking drawing, dictating, conversing, writing, and class content and knowledge. Sophia also learned to see valuable connections between early writing and children's sense of themselves as competent learners and writers, the value of structured opportunities to support English learners as they begin to write, and the benefits of inquiry as a form of assessment—"Since I now see that children are able to draw with more detail and clarity than they can speak, I can look at a writing sample about a given topic and see what a child knows." The inquiry process also offered insights for moving Sophia forward in her journey as a relatively new teacher—to learn "more about how to be more strategic in my abilities to nudge students to the next level of writing development without pushing them to frustration," to start "more conventional writing for students with the skill sets," and to teach "families about the importance of writing and how to give them the skills to help their children."

Understanding and Improving Student Writing—NaNoWriMo in Fifth Grade

Bob Garrison is in his seventh year teaching fifth grade in the Berkeley Unified School District. For the last three years, his classes have participated in a national nonprofit's writing activity called the National Novel Writing Month, or NaNoWriMo (http://nanowrimo.org/), which occurs each year for the month of November. Bob discovered NaNoWriMo from his own children's elementary school's afterschool program, and he was amazed to discover that one student had written a novel that he actually self-published. For the last three years that he has implemented NaNoWriMo in his classroom, Bob has shown that student's self-published novel and told his class that they too have the ability write their own novel and to self-publish—"I see that this starts a spark in the students, and I like knowing that they have the opportunity to do something like self-publish a novel through their NaNoWriMo experience."

Three years ago, Bob was the only teacher at his grade level who did NaNoWriMo at his school; the second year one other colleague joined him, and for the third and most recent year Bob was joined by another colleague so that all three fifth-grade teachers participated. The NaNoWriMo organization encourages students to write a "novel" of their own creation, and provides support in terms of visuals online to record students' word count goals, and also "trophy badges" at the end of the month's writing. Bob's students can choose their own writing partners, write their shared story in Google Docs using Chrome computers at school, and peer edit their joint novel. Students also have the freedom to write their novel out of school on their own computers or at the library.

In his most current NaNoWriMo implementation, Bob affixed a NaNoWriMo poster on the classroom's front whiteboard that lists each partner group's names, their word count goal, and a bar graph showing their current percentage toward reaching their word count goal. (In his first year of NaNoWriMo implementation, Bob made his own poster that only tracked word count and in the last two years he has used the poster provided by the NaNoWriMo organization.) After the first week of NaNoWriMo, Bob had each partner group set their own goal for the end of the month, and Bob checked their word count every few days and the students updated their bar graph each week to track their progress. Bob has seen how the poster provides a motivating visual for all students, as they track their bar graph and percentage toward their word count goal. Since the word count goal varies by team, the bar graph can look visually competitive across all teams so that the students with lower writing skills don't become discouraged seeing classmates outperform them, which can happen if Bob only tracked the actual word count. Before the month ended, each team created their book cover with the book title, authors' names, and an exciting image that captured the theme of their book. At the end of November, each student partnership shared a portion of their novel with the whole class during the classroom's publishing party. The novels were then kept in a box and students chose each other's novels as part of their independent reading each morning.

In looking at the students' NaNoWriMo writing, and in talking with grade-level colleagues, Bob now more clearly sees the benefits of NaNoWriMo for his students' writing development, and also how NaNoWriMo supports his overall philosophy and curriculum for teaching writing. Bob sees how NaNoWriMo's placement in November is a beneficial change of writing genre after the small moment and persuasive writing (his district follows the Teachers College Reading & Writing Project) that students worked on in the earlier grades and continue at the start of fifth grade (B. Garrison, personal communication, January 14, 2016).

Bob also now sees NaNoWriMo as occurring at an important point in the narrative arc of his yearlong writing program. It precedes a large research writing project that Bob begins in January, which is a long-term writing project in which students research an aspect of early American history, take notes on their topic, create an outline, and then write multiple drafts of their research paper. NaNoWriMo helps with the research project since it builds writing "endurance and quantity" for the students' subsequent long-term and multi-step research report work in January. Bob views NaNoWriMo as "an opportunity for students to express themselves and to fall in love with writing. They beg to do this writing each day. It allows students to tap into their creativity and their imagination, and they also get a chance to write at home."

Bob now has three years of writing data to consider as he reflects on NaNoWriMo's benefits as well as its problematic aspects. For instance, he has noticed that the students' choice of their own writing partners most often results in partners of similar writing skills and abilities. Bob has observed that for the students who are more skilled and knowledgeable writers, NaNoWriMo is a "more open-ended and creative writing activity" that encourages the more "independent and knowledgeable students to write more at their own pace, and to become engaged, passionate, and to feel good about their writing. They are not held back in any way."

For students with mid-level writing skills and knowledge, NaNoWriMo offered them a new opportunity for "stretching themselves as writers by working for a whole month on a topic that interested them." Bob reflected that this group of students was more productive than when Bob "pushes a genre" in other parts of the writing curriculum. "It's particularly hard," Bob argues, "for the middle-range students and those most in need of writing support to write a "small moment story about space travel or something related to *Harry Potter*," since students are expected to write about small moments that actually happened to them.

But for the third group of students, those most in need of writing support and who partnered with each other, Bob has noticed that these groups floundered more than those partners with at least one "high" or "mid-level" writer. So in the third year of NaNoWriMo, Bob tried to change the plotline for this group of student writers most in need, sitting with the partner groups and helping brainstorm their ideas for their novel's direction, and taking their dictation as Bob directly typed into their Google document. By the third year of providing this level of support, Bob realized it was too time-consuming for him, and actually detracted from his goal of promoting independent writing and the students writing on their own. In terms of possible next instructional steps for next year, Bob will select each partner group for all the students to ensure more of a mix of writing abilities and knowledge, and to carefully select partners who will work well with each other.

Bob's three years of work with NaNoWriMo illustrates a few key elements of narrative inquiry as seen in a long-term writing project. First, in terms of the initial provocation for instructional change, Bob started the NaNoWriMo writing three years ago because of the power of one student's self-published novel. It was the curricular spark, the story starter, that hooked Bob into developing a new process and product for deepening his writing curriculum. Second, in looking at the temporal arc of Bob's writing program over the course of the year, Bob now sees NaNoWriMo as occurring at an effective teaching and learning point in the year. It's a welcome change of pace from other forms of genre writing and serves as effective preparation for the research project writing following NaNoWriMo. Third, in terms of the learning arc of his students' writing development, NaNoWriMo provides a burst of creative and imaginative writing energy, encouraging his students to write collaboratively with a partner, and to experiment with written language content and mechanics in a new writing genre. Fourth, looking back over the three years of NaNoWriMo implementation, Bob now more clearly sees multiple teaching and learning plotlines, as well as certain instructional tensions to be resolved as he moves forward.

The Literacy Achievement of African-American Male Students—Fifth Grade

Kirsti Jewel Peters-Hoyte (2015), in a Mills Teacher Scholars blog post (http://millsscholars.org/shifting-my-thinking-shifting-their-achievement-an-asset-approach-to-supporting-african-american-male-readers/), examined the reading achievement of three of her fifth-grade African-American male students. Kirsti wanted to find a counter-story to what she considered a worn-out refrain or dominant narrative—since African-American boys operate from a deficit in their language and literacy learning, they don't have the talents and abilities to read and write well.

> I was tired, and I continue to be tired, of discussions around African American boys from a deficit lens. And I've grown tired of the excuses that are spouted off in response to these statistics: *They have tough homes. They just won't listen. They can't stay in the classroom. They just can't focus. They don't like reading.* (original emphasis)

To upend this persistent perspective and dominant narrative, Kirsti gave herself a new inquiry plotline or provocation from a strength-based approach—"How *are* my African-American boys responding to literature through writing?" Kirsti carefully chose the students' pseudonyms—Amiri Baraka, Langston Hughes, and Alvin Ailey.

Kirsti examined the three students' weekly, three-paragraph letters (Calkins, 2006) in which they summarized their book, discussed key passages of interest, and provided their opinion of the text and recommendations for other readers. In examining their letters, Kirsti specifically looked for and found evidence of positive changes in the students' skill transfer from their reading, textual engagement and interest, understanding of content, and the ability to discuss their reading with peers and Kirsti.

Kirsti wanted to change the narrative arc of her students' engagement and learning in terms of their motivation for literacy engagement, depth of literacy understanding and knowledge, and literary performance for self and others. In essence, Kirsti sought a new identity for the students in terms of their own views of themselves as readers, writers, and thinkers within the forum of the classroom community. So Kirsti made a few specific instructional changes to guide the three boys in new teaching and learning directions, and hoping for a new kind of trajectory or narrative arc for the students' literacy education.

> I thought deeply about how I could engage my students and tried to be strategic with the books I chose. The first book that the boys read in their book club was one that featured a boy who loved baseball, was the class clown, and was running for Class President. I soon realized, however, that neither Baraka or Carmichael found the story compelling, and, at times, didn't even complete assignments. I knew that Amiri Baraka and Stokely Carmichael were critical thinkers who were able to make strong connections with stories and the real world, and I wondered if the story was too simple for them, so the next book I chose was *Esperanza Rising* by Pam Munoz Ryan. When we began reading, I noticed a difference in their excitement for book club, and because the book dealt with difficult topics, their thinking and, eventually, their writing became more complex. *Esperanza Rising* didn't directly address issues within the African American community, but the students could still connect with the book. As a class, we were learning about both the Civil Rights Movement and the Black Panther Party, and they were able to make connections with themes from *Esperanza Rising* and their own personal experiences. (K. J. Peters-Hoyte, personal communication, January 22, 2016)

As part of this narrative inquiry journey, and in the culminating public blog forum through Mills Teacher Scholars, Kirsti wanted to publicize and recognize the linguistic and literary talents of African-American students, hers and others.

She also wanted her blog post, as the public product of her narrative inquiry work, to link her three students' literacy achievements as an expression of solidarity with both the historical challenges and successes of other African-American children.

> As a nation, there are low expectations for what African Americans are doing and for who they, eventually, will be. When I look at my students, I like to imagine who they will be when they're adults—what will their professions be? What will they do for the world? I also like to remember that our most famous icons—people like Amiri Baraka, Langston Hughes, and Alvin Ailey—were once children who may have struggled in school. They may or may not have had nurturing educators in their life who supported them, just as they may have had teachers who failed them. For our future activists, writers, and professional dancers, I hope that I'm an educator that supports them in their educational experience. (K. J. Peters-Hoyte, personal communication, January 22, 2016)

Kirsti sees narrative inquiry as a powerful form of storytelling, which she personally defines as "a style of passing down information that responds to me culturally. I connect most with storytellers, my grandmother was a storyteller, and the most brilliant minds know how to tell a good story."

Just as important as seeing a new narrative arc for her students' writing skills and knowledge, Kirsti afforded herself a new plotline for her teaching and professional growth—"Because I was intentional about focusing on what my students could do, rather than what they weren't doing, I was able to highlight their strengths for myself, and reflect back onto my students." Her own professional writing and literacy, as captured in her observational notes and in her blog post, allowed Kirsti to "process and analyze" her "craft," and to become more "cognizant" of her "professional growth." The writing, as a parallel professional story to her students, deepened Kirsti's understanding of how and why she made effective changes in her teaching—"writing is a meditative practice that allows potentially fleeting learning experiences to become something more solid, allowing me to consciously shift my practice as an educator."

As an epilogue to her project, but as part of her continuing journey of self-reflection, Kirsti now sees an important way that her narrative inquiry could have been strengthened.

> One of the things that teachers want to know is what does culturally relevant pedagogy look like in the classroom. I think this is a tough question, because it can look different in many ways, but I wish that, in my blog post, I had explicitly named that the philosophy that I took when approaching my students, was a culturally responsive stance. From the mindset that I consciously set for myself, to the books that I chose, to the ways that

I engaged families—this all came from a culturally responsive lens. My high expectations that I held for my students, while also adjusting to their needs, was also an example of culturally responsive pedagogy. I don't think you can truly support students of color to reach their absolute full potential without taking a culturally responsive approach, and I think that's very important to name.

In initially giving her three students powerful pseudonyms (Amiri Baraka, Langston Hughes, and Alvin Ailey), Kirsti started her project with the idea that the language and terms that we use in our professional inquiry stories influences the content of our message, and thus how we wish to affect our audiences. In recognizing, post-project and post-blog, that explicitly linking the three students' literacy achievements as connected to elements of culturally responsive teaching, Kirsti now even more deeply recognizes the power of language (for characters, place, plot) for well-told and transformative professional stories.

Closing

As language and literacy instruction becomes ever more complicated—with new technologies, increased standards, expanded curricular expectations, increased assessments—we need more sophisticated inquiry tools to understand children's language and literacy development, and to strengthen and improve our educational practices. The theory and practical examples presented and discussed in this chapter offer food for thought about how to meet this challenge. As argued and shown here, narrative inquiry has the potential for sharpening our observational lenses, tightening our documentation strategies, and deepening our reflection and analysis of student learning and instructional practices. The narrative inquiry work profiled here—Daniel's project on read-alouds and journals in preschool, Rachel's work on multilingualism in preschool, Sophia's project on drawing and early writing in transitional kindergarten, Bob's work on writing in fifth grade, and Kirsti's project on reading and writing in fifth grade—all point to the power of story as a central way to stop instructional time, and to rewind the "tape" of our teaching to see our most effective points of teaching and engagement. This process of looking back also helps us look forward, giving us new ideas and next steps for both instruction and inquiry.

7

PULLING IT ALL TOGETHER

Narrative Inquiry in Action

One of the challenges that teachers face in making narrative inquiry part of their practice is that most examples of narrative inquiry research are *not* teacher conducted. While narrative inquiry studies *about* classrooms, children, teachers, and curriculum often draw teachers to this methodology, it soon becomes clear that conducting inquiry while also teaching presents both challenges and perspectives that differ quite significantly from those encountered by university researchers or anyone else who is not simultaneously engaging in research and coordinating the teaching and learning environment for a dozen or more children. Often, when teachers are drawn to the idea of narrative inquiry, uncomfortable questions inhibit them from jumping in: What does a "finished" narrative inquiry look like? Where do I even start? How do I decide what narratives to collect? Won't I be overwhelmed with stories as data? How do I move from just telling and collecting stories to using them as an inquiry into teaching and learning? Does this really count as research?

The earlier chapters of this book take up many core issues of narrative inquiry, and we have sought to provide perspectives, tools, and practices to make the process of narrative inquiry both compelling and accessible for classroom teachers. However, like other teachers, we understand the power of a model in helping to conceptualize what "finished" might look like. And so in this chapter, we present a paper written by Michael Escamilla, a full time preschool teacher who is also a gifted narrative inquirer. Examples of his inquiry work have appeared in small glimpses in earlier chapters. Here, he offers a more complete account of his inquiry into how his young students engaged in and integrated learning experiences in the classroom with those outside the classroom walls, at a local museum, and at the nearby bay.

We offer Michael's account of his inquiry not as a script for engaging in narrative inquiry, as the specifics of one's teaching environment and lived experiences so deeply influence the form and outcomes of this methodology. Rather, we use this as an opportunity to consider how deliberately collected stories of teaching can be organized and analyzed to provide insight into the teaching and learning process. Certain features of this account make it a particularly good model of narrative inquiry that is completely integrated into other aspects of teaching practice, thus making the process of narrative inquiry a part of the everyday work of teaching rather than an "extra" activity to be done only when required by graduate studies or formal professional development efforts.

Michael's narrative inquiry is clearly *organized around a core question or puzzle of practice*. He wants to explore how children, teachers, and parents "(re)connect with nature and discover the principles of scientific inquiry through hands-on activities." Thus, the stories and other documentation he draws upon are those that bring to life the participants' experiences in his specific efforts to add a nature-based component to his curriculum. Michael regularly keeps a teacher journal, takes photos of children's activities, and keeps notes about conversations with parents and colleagues. But the shift from "reflective practice" to "narrative inquiry" requires zooming in on a subset of stories and interactions directly relevant to his current puzzle of practice.

Michael's inquiry *places emphasis on the social and relational aspects of learning*, those that are often best captured by narrative approaches (Johnson & Golombek, 2002). While he could collect data around his question in a wide variety of ways, for instance through analyzing work samples for evidence of understanding or through quantifying the amount of time children spend in nature-oriented activities before and after different interventions, he chooses instead to focus on the ways in which child and adult participants relate to each other and to the natural world, capturing "small moments" of classroom life and retold stories of connection and disconnection from nature in people's lives in and out of school. In other words, part of what makes this narrative inquiry is the decision to focus on *narrative* as the primary data that is collected and on *stories of people in relation to one another* as the unit of analysis.

Michael's inquiry avoids the dangers of a single story by *deliberately inviting, collecting, and seeking to learn from the stories of diverse participants*, in this case teachers, students, and adult family members. His classroom includes children whose families come from many parts of the world, and the adult family members have widely varying past experiences with nature. By collecting and honoring these family stories, he is able to build a more complete understanding of how the children in his class make meaning of nature-based experiences in their own lives. Part of this process involves the interweaving of personal, "non-school" stories with narratives of school experiences, with the goal of examining how characters' whole lives inform and create their lived experiences in school. While collecting multiple stories in multiple settings will not necessarily widen our own understanding, *deliberately seeking counter-narratives*, as Michael does in eliciting experiences of parents, children, and his teaching colleagues, reduces the risk that the researcher will only attend to stories that fit his or her existing ideas.

Finally, Michael *uses multiple forms of documentation* to offer diverse perspectives and tell the complex story of teaching and learning. While "story" forms the basic structure of data collection in narrative inquiry, those stories are informed by a wide variety of documentation, including: direct transcription of conversations, photographs of participants engaged in activities, students' work (in Michael's inquiry, children's artwork is the primary example of this), teachers' journals, sequential descriptions of core activities related to the inquiry question, and the written and spoken reflections of multiple participants. Michael has developed the habit of collecting copious documentation of children and families interacting with each other and with classroom materials, and he is able to pull from this record of classroom life to develop a multi-faceted narrative of different participants' engagement with nature.

As you read Michael's account, consider how this approach might become part of your everyday teaching practice. We encourage you to consider narrative inquiry as an approach to understanding teaching and learning and as a means to keep the focus of teaching on the puzzles and problems that are most important to the particular teacher(s) and children in a classroom.

DOCUMENTING SCHOOL AND COMMUNITY LEARNING EXPERIENCES

By Michael Escamilia, Las Americas Preschool

Three years ago my preschool began a partnership with the Bay Area Discovery Museum, located near the Golden Gate Bridge in Sausalito, with five scheduled field trips to the museum throughout the year to support children, teachers, and parents to (re)connect with nature and discover the principles of scientific inquiry through hands-on activities (Figure 7.1). To start our new partnership with the Bay Area Discovery Museum we hosted a parents' evening for families to meet the museum staff and learn about the proposed program. The museum's Connections Program coordinators used this opportunity to gain knowledge of the children's and parents' prior experiences to better adapt the program to suit their interests. Parents shared heartfelt stories of their childhood and the role that nature played in their games, imagination, creativity, growth, relationships, and personal identity. For example, Daniel's mom remembered that as a child living in Nicaragua she used to go out with her grandmother to their backyard garden where she learned to recognize the healing properties of different herbs. Amy's father shared with the group a story of how he used to play with handmade toys on the seashore of his hometown in Mexico.

During our parents' get-together with the museum staff we agreed that the goal of the first field trip to the museum was to familiarize children, teachers, and parents with this unique museum environment where children are actively encouraged to touch, explore, and discover at their own pace. The parents enjoyed the first field trip to the Bay Area Discovery Museum and happily joined the children in exploring the nature trails around the Laboratory Garden (Figure 7.2). They relaxed amid the eucalyptus trees and encouraged the children to rub the leaves and fill their lungs with their sweet fragrance. The adults seemed to like this nature walk as much as the children and Isaac's mom exclaimed, "It's been a long time since I was in a place where you can breathe fresh air that smells like pine cones."

FIGURE 7.1 Approaching the Bay Area Discovery Museum. [Photo credit: Michael Escamilla]

FIGURE 7.2 Parent and children exploring nature. [Photo credit: Michael Escamilla]

When children, parents, and teachers share a common experience it sets the context in which all of us can exchange ideas, make comments, or simply reminisce about the events that took place that day. For example, after the first visit to the museum some children talked about how big and beautiful the Golden Gate Bridge looked, while others focused on the hide-and-seek game they played in the garden-lab and the giant tree stump where they found the best hiding spot. The photographs we took during our first trip, which we later displayed in the classroom, provided a reference point from which we could start a casual conversation that sometimes led to an in-depth dialogue between children, between children and teachers, or between teachers and parents, and most certainly between parents and children. Back in the classroom, when we asked Manuel to tell us what he remembered about the excursion, he said, "*A mi me gusto mas jugar en el barco y también me gusto porque mi mama fué conmigo. Me gusto donde nos escondimos con Angel y con Miriam.*" ("I pretty much enjoyed playing in the ship and I also enjoyed that my mom was with me. It was also fun when we played hide-and-seek with Angel and Miriam.")

In one of our extension activities, a letter addressed to the parents asked them to help their children to collect natural things to bring to school. The children discovered that the leaves on a tree, the feathers of a bird, the flowers in a garden, or the seaweed on the seashore is all part of nature. When we opened the brown bags containing the children's nature objects, the children were very excited to see the treasures each one of them brought to school and they told stories about of how they got those items. They brought shiny pebbles, patterned shells, and wood chips among many other things, which they classified by shape, color, or texture. The children were particularly intrigued to see that corn comes in different colors: purple, yellow, white, or mixed. They also learned that the dry leaves are called corn husks. From this activity they had the idea of planting corn in the garden and we promised we would be doing just that the first day of spring.

A few children brought small orange pumpkins or red pomegranates, which they put in a basket to play and share with their friends. We placed our natural treasures on display to make a pretend store. In the store the children sell pinecones, feathers, sea shells, small pumpkins, big pumpkins, leaves, pebbles, and many more beautiful things.

Excerpt from a teacher's journal:

> The pretend store is very popular and everyone wants a turn selling, but the children have learned that not everyone can be the seller at the same time. Sometimes conflicts happen and they have to negotiate to find a solution. They are learning to take turns and they seem to understand

*that only one person can be the seller while the others can be the custom-
ers. When the children pretend to be customers and want to buy something, they wait in line. Selling and buying are lots of fun for them. When
the children are done playing they simply put all their natural treasures
back on the shelves.*

Since the children had a lot to say about corn, we then collected their stories
as proof of their base knowledge on the topic. We used the children's dicta-
tions to analyze the use of their home language in meaningful conversations
and to find ways to support their emergent interest in learning more about
how to grow corn in our schoolyard garden. These stories guided us toward
choosing a topic that offers multiple possibilities to learn early concepts of
math, science, literacy, and art.

At the children's insistence we planted a few corn kernels in the school
garden in the middle of the winter, which did not offer the best climate
conditions for this type of sun-loving plants. To our surprise and to the
children's delight, a few sprouts found their way out of the damp cold soil
guided by the occasional dim sunlight. With the children's constant care of

---

**Miriam's Story
Dictated in Spanish**

Los elotes se compran en la
tienda. Mi mama los com-
pra ahí y después hace sopa.
A mí me gustan mucho los
elotes. También vamos a
comer elotes en la escuela
ya que estén grande los que
plantamos allá afuera en el
jardín.

*You buy corn at the store. My
mom buys them there and
then she makes soup. I like
corn a lot. We are going to eat
corn at school when the ones
we planted out in the garden
get big.*

**Isaac's Story
Dictated in English**

You buy corn at the store.
Also people sell corn in the
street and at the park. My
dad buys me corn on the
cob with mayonnaise but
he likes his with lemon and
spicy chili and my mom with
just a lot of chili.

*Los elotes los compran en la
tienda. También los señores
venden elotes allá en la calle
y en el parque. Mi papa me
compra elotes con mayonesa.
A el le gusta con chile y limón
y a mi mama con mucho
chile.*

the plants, some grew and the project culminated in the harvesting of a few corn ears that we boiled for the children to eat as snack one afternoon.

Reflection in Action—Class Field Trip to the Bay Area Discovery Museum

A few days before our field trip to the Bay Area Discovery Museum where the children would have the opportunity to go down to the beach near the Golden Gate Bridge, they made a collage with tissue paper in various shades of blue to represent the water they expected to see (Figure 7.3). In preparation for our beach outing we made a list of items we would bring with us: sandals, shorts, sunblock, pails, scoops, shovels, buckets, and small toy boats. For our field trip the children had anticipated the weather to be hot and sunny. Instead, the day was somewhat cloudy and even a little cool. When we got there, the water in the bay was rather grey, in sharp contrast with the turquoise blue tissue paper collage the children had created the week before.

The magnificent Golden Gate Bridge was shrouded in a veil of mist and fog. Elvis exclaimed *Hey! The Golden Gate Bridge is in the clouds!* And Daniel asked *Where is the bridge? Where is the top of the bridge? I only see clouds . . .* The children had seen the bridge up close a few times before, but this time it looked different. We took a photograph to keep the memory (Figure 7.4).

Zoe and Nasley, our museum field trip guides, read a storybook to our class about Swimmy, a little fish in the deep sea where there is a world full of wonders (Figure 7.5). This story opened the children's minds to the imagination and to the possible animals that they too could come across on our field trip. We invited the children to predict the animals they could find in our walk. We made a list of creatures they thought they would see and at the end of the exploration

FIGURE 7.3   Making a water collage before the visit. [Photo credit: Michael Escamilla]

FIGURE 7.4   First moments observing the bridge. [Photo credit: Michael Escamilla]

FIGURE 7.5   Listening to a story. [Photo credit: Michael Escamilla]

we revised the list to tally the animals we actually saw. Back in our school the children reviewed the photographs to refresh their memory, relive the field trip, and make representations of what they considered important.

Mary Lin, one of the teachers on this field trip, considers that this type of outdoor experience offers our children, who live in such an urban environment, the opportunity to interact with and feel a part of nature. According to Alicia Alvarez, another one of the teachers, the value of this experience is that children can actually see for themselves a lot of natural things around them and it is in this real context that the children add new words to their vocabulary. Some of those words the children learned this time are goose, geese, and gosling, thanks to a family of geese we saw nearby. At first, the children referred to them as ducks, but upon further discussion and observation they discovered that they were not ducks, but geese (Figure 7.6).

For teacher Edwin Serrano, this vast body of water was the perfect place to run a little experiment and test what items could sink and what items could float. For example, one of the children, Fetuali'i, noticed that a piece of driftwood, no matter how big, floats, and a rock, no matter how small, sinks.

For Aldo, one of the younger children, the water and the returning waves gave him the idea to build a canal or burrow, like the ones they had built back in our schoolyard sandbox when they played with the toy boats, but now he had a much bigger space in which to play, explore, and learn (Figure 7.7). With so many pebbles and rocks all around us, some of the children tried to count them while collecting them in their pails. This was a math activity we had not anticipated would happen. The same way that teacher Sahara Gonzalez did not anticipate that 5-year-old Mauricio would discover a tiny crab, which led him to formulate this theory: "Crabs hide under rocks from the water so that the water don't pull them away." Mauricio continued with his theory adding, "Although crabs can swim too, they don't want to and they want to sleep under the rocks." When children are exposed to different exciting environments that break the routine of their everyday life they wonder, ask questions, explore, investigate, discover, and make connections. For example, Mauricio concluded by saying that the word "crab" starts with letter C and in doing so, he made a connection to what he's been learning in class.

When our exploration ended we returned to our school in the city with memories of a great day by the bay. Since the Golden Gate Bridge is the last thing we saw, it left a big impression on the children and they painted a bridge as an extension activity of such an exciting field trip (Figure 7.8). Drawing the bridge presented some technical challenges to the children,

FIGURE 7.6 The children observe geese. [Photo credit: Michael Escamilla]

FIGURE 7.7   Interacting with sand and water at the museum. [Photo credit: Michael Escamilla]

FIGURE 7.8   Painting the bridge. [Photo credit: Michael Escamilla]

but working as a team and with the right adult support they found solutions and seemed proud of their final rendition. Although the Golden Gate Bridge was not initially envisioned by teachers as part of the water investigation, the children's interest and their motivation to draw it somehow made it fit in with the rest of the activities; after all, it is the water in the bay what led to its construction and according to Manuel "si no hay agua no se necesita el puente" meaning *if there's no water, there's no need for the bridge.*

To recreate their bridge, the children used a variety of writing materials such as pencils, pens, markers, paintbrushes, watercolors, and tempera paint. In terms of materials, they also used tissue paper, watercolor paper, and construction paper. In the process, they learned that there are different kinds of paper and each one of them has its own purpose and use. It took several days to complete the painting. One day, when we left it outside to air dry, a light rain came down, smearing paint all over the paper. In the end it worked out just fine, but some paint strokes were not intentional; especially the sunset tones in the background. These are the result of raindrops, which in a certain way only add character to the children's painting (Figure 7.9).

When the bridge was finally done, Elvis and Manuel realized that the bridge was missing something very important: cars. So, they started sketching again and created a new bridge; this time with traffic in the form of car cutouts going north. In the children's version of the bridge the traffic goes one way only (Figure 7.10). The reason for this, according to Elvis, was to avoid accidents.

From our teachers' perspective, the children's drawing of the bridge is more than a graphic representation of the Golden Gate Bridge. It is a symbolic representation of the connections between the busy city streets of the Mission District of San Francisco and the lush hills of Sausalito, connections between the teachers of Las Americas Early Education School and the dedicated staff of the Bay Area Discovery Museum. It represents the connections being made between teachers and parents and between parents and children in a shared common experience.

FIGURE 7.9 The Golden Gate Bridge. [Photo credit: Michael Escamilla]

FIGURE 7.10   The Golden Gate Bridge with cars going one way. [Photo credit: Michael Escamilla]

Perhaps our favorite bridge symbol, though, is that of hope. If you can just get over that bridge, you may find yourself in a better place on the other side. True, some bridges are harder to cross than others. So, in some ways bridges can represent a struggle, but one with the prospect of better things on the far shore. Manuel, Crystal, and Aldo might simply view the bridge as the only way to reach a destination but even if that is the case, the bridge then becomes an obstacle that has to be overcome. Once on the other side, they've arrived! Metaphorically speaking, they have conquered one of the many bridges they will encounter in life. And as teachers of young children, we find that inspiring.

These are but two examples of the kind of documentation that we present in our inquiry group meetings. Since there were five trips to the museum over the course of one year, we had multiple opportunities to collect data and to reflect on the meaning of our documentation in our meetings. Our inquiry group provides a stable forum for us to share our individual perspectives on these projects, as well as others, and to receive affirmation, recognition, and reflections for the value of our inquiry-based teaching and learning.

8

NARRATIVE INQUIRY AND EDUCATIONAL CHANGE

> The children wanted to memorize certain poems and rhymes that required some amount of practice, and so I kept returning to Nina Crews' *Neighborhood Mother Goose*. And there were the unexpected books that both the children and I enjoyed. I came across Benji Davies' *The Storm Whale*, a story about a young child who cares for a whale found on the beach, and then releases the whale back to the ocean with his father. After reading it twice two weeks in a row, we all rejoiced at the story's closing—"Noi often thought about the storm whale. He hoped that one day, soon . . . he would see his friend again." And he does. (Meier, unpublished narrative-based observational notes)

We close the book with a discussion on how narrative is a powerful tool for increasing teachers' sense of agency, and how narrative-based tools and ways of thinking and acting can influence our adaptability and flexibility. We propose, as in Daniel's narrative snippet above, that focusing on narrative and inquiry helps teachers adapt to the ever-changing curricular landscape in education, and to make strong professional choices in an age of a dizzying arena of external standards and accountability measures. And as teachers continue to be left out of the conceptualization and implementation of reform efforts, teachers need more sophisticated and varied ways for understanding and acting upon the often chaotic and haphazard imposition of standards, assessments, technologies, and "best practices."

Narrative Inquiry—Tools and Goals

The stories presented in this book—ours and those of the dedicated and talented early childhood and elementary school educators—showcase the value of pursuing narrative inquiry work in a range of forms and for varied purposes. The narrative inquiry work that we have presented illuminates the range of narrative forms and tools that we can employ in narrative inquiry. The material that we presented describes how various tools—diaries and journal accounts, observational notes, audiorecording, videotaping, photography, blogging, and others—offer us a resourceful toolbox for starting and extending narrative inquiry work in classrooms and schools.

For example, Daniel used observational notes to document and tell the small stories each week of the preschoolers' language and literacy experiences and learning. Stephanie described the value of video for children's self-interviews about their science learning, and explains how this medium captures children's anecdotes and stories with immediacy and visual power, and can reach multiple, distant audiences. Michael Escamilla, the preschool teacher in San Francisco featured in Chapters 3 and 7, used photography to capture and document his children's nature and outdoor experiences, such as his story of the children's trip to a local science museum, and how the children integrated nature, science, multilingualism, and art to deepen the meaning of their experiences. Renetta Goeson, the early childhood administrator from South Dakota discussed in Chapter 3, used a variety of texts (stories and interviews), photographs (archival photographs from museums and historical societies), and original art to create a moving narrative that honors her Native American ancestors, and offers a passionate vision for the power of remembering social and educational injustices for social and educational renewal and change. Kirsti Jewel Peters-Hoyte, who taught fifth grade and is featured in Chapter 5, wanted to find a new narrative path to understand and recognize the talents of her African-American boys, and documented three students' (whom she called Amiri Baraka, Langston Hughes, and Alvin Ailey) reading and writing activities, and in the process found a new plotline for shifting her teaching knowledge and practices. And other educators who are dedicated narrative inquirers in our book offer their own constellation of narrative inquiry tools to advance their personal and professional goals and strengthen their teaching and leadership.

For novice narrative inquirers, we encourage you to pick and choose those narrative inquiry tools that make for a successful and "doable" start to your inquiry work. Perhaps you would like to start on your own, not working with a colleague at the outset, and select one or two tools and a small focus for inquiry. For instance, using photography is a relatively quick and logistically doable approach for capturing children's interactions and moments-in-learning that can highlight key narrative moments, points of tension, and points of resolution. Daniel, in the graduate school class he teaches on narrative inquiry and memoir, asks the teacher participants to create a photo story of a child or children engaged in learning over a certain time period. For instance, one teacher chronicled a preschool child jumping off a large rock outside over the course of 10 minutes. Many photographs can be taken, and then a selection of 10 to 12 photo "gems" can be arranged to tell a small teaching and learning story, which often tells a larger story of engagement, learning, and development.

For experienced educators and narrative inquirers, choosing a more involved focus and a range of narrative inquiry tools will extend one's inquiry work in professionally satisfying ways. Collaboration with colleagues at your school or site, or even with educators at other sites, often serves to broaden and enliven the narrative inquiry journey, offering multiple perspectives on the stories collected and shared. For instance, Daniel collected his preschool data and met regularly with another veteran teacher, Louise Rosenkranz, who also conducted whole-group read-alouds and small-group literacy work at another preschool in the same public school district. Daniel and Louise met on a regular basis to compare observational notes, photographs, and samples of student work. They also shared articles on narrative inquiry and children's language and literacy work, which deepened their inquiry discussions by pushing the "narrative envelope" of their individual and collective narrative inquiry. In addition, in another layer of narrative inquiry collaboration and dialogue, Daniel and Louise were also in contact internationally via email and Skype with Dr. Majida Dajani, a teacher educator and teacher working in the West Bank, Palestine. Dr. Dajani worked with local teachers on narrative inquiry and children's narrative development in English and Arabic in reading and writing. The ongoing opportunity to compare data from the San Francisco Bay area schools with Dr. Dajani's students and teachers offered another level of storytelling and perspective-taking around children's language and literacy learning, and new inquiry paths for using narrative inquiry in varied social, educational, and cultural settings.

Narrative Inquiry—Personal and Professional Transformation

As the co-authors of this text, we embarked on a new narrative journey, as we learned new ways to understand each other's teaching, writing, and experiences with and understanding of narrative inquiry in teaching and educational change. In this process, we exchanged the small and large stories of our teaching histories, and our views and knowledge of the potential power of narrative inquiry for educational change and transformation. On a personal and professional note, this process benefitted us both, challenging us to reconsider and reshape not only our understanding of narrative inquiry as a field and a professional pursuit, but as a way for our individual stories and paths to meet, sometimes blending in harmony, sometimes not, and resulting in a measure of asynchrony. This is what happens when narrative inquiry is pursued with others—our personal and professional stories deepen in their sacredness for us and also shift as we listen to and engage with the others' stories.

We are at a critical point—a challenge and an opportunity—in early childhood and elementary education where the demands (policy, instruction, assessment, curriculum) are outstripping the time, energy, and resources at our disposal for truly understanding and improving our teaching and learning as professionals. While we have an unprecedented array of technological tools and resources that we might potentially use to investigate and document our teaching, we suffer from a lack of time and institutional understanding and support for sustained, home-grown professional growth and development. We argue, based on the theory, ideas, practice, and examples provided in this book, that narrative inquiry—when done well and done in concert with colleagues—offers a fruitful new path, a new set of plotlines, for improving our understanding of engaged student learning and achievement, personal and professional growth for teachers, and institutional change and adaptability.

To move forward in these fruitful directions, from a policy and leadership perspective, we need acknowledgment of narrative inquiry as a viable avenue for documentation, assessment, teacher knowledge, and professional growth. For those in positions of influence and resource allocation, promoting an interest and investment in narrative inquiry can come from on high, and also from the "bottom-up," as advocates of narrative inquiry in schools are supported with new directions and resources in instruction, curriculum, assessment, and professional development.

This can happen in a number of ways. In the field of early childhood education, the small independent infant/toddler and preschool sites can adopt small measures and elements of narrative inquiry as a way to begin. For instance, teachers can be encouraged and supported to take regular observational notes—looking for a good teaching–learning story to tell—and to share these notes with colleagues at regular faculty meetings. The large early childhood centers, such as Bright Horizons and Head Start and others, might incorporate elements of narrative inquiry in their assessment measures, asking teachers for instance to document small moments of learning that illustrate certain levels of mastery and development. For this to happen, of course, the standardized assessment measures used by these large constellations of early childhood centers need to be adapted and changed to include elements of narrative inquiry.

At the elementary school level, district-wide professional days each year can include training in narrative inquiry goals, tools, and strategies both for novice and veteran teachers, and to be integrated across the range of content areas. For this to happen, administrators at the district level must become more knowledge-able consumers of narrative inquiry theory and practice, and to figure out ways to distill key elements of narrative inquiry for the typically infrequent professional development days in most school districts. Further, as more districts and schools adopt forms for professional learning communities (PLCs), this might well prove the most efficient avenue for slipping in elements of narrative inquiry as a form of professional growth and development. For instance, if teachers are reading and discussing a shared text in their PLCs, then the idea of teachers sharing their personal stories and stories based on systematic documentation and reflection can be included to deepen the discussion, and make important connections from text to practice.

Closing—Trusting Our Stories, Trusting Our Words

The poet Garrett Hongo, in an excerpt from his poem "What For," reminds us of the power of words for conjuring new ideas and feelings and connections to magic, to others, and to the earth.

> At six I lived for spells:
> how a few Hawaiian words could call
> up the rain, could hymn like the sea
> in the long swirl of chambers
> curling in the nautilus of a shell,
> how Amida's ballads of the Buddhaland
> in the drone of the priest's liturgy
> could conjure money from the poor
> and give them nothing but mantras,
> the strange syllables that healed desire.
>
> I lived for stories about the war
> my grandfather told over *hana* cards,
> slapping them down on the mats
> with a sharp Japanese *kiai*.
>
> I lived for songs my grandmother sang
> stirring curry into a thick stew,
> weaving a calligraphy of Kannon's love
> into grass mats and straw sandals.
> (reprinted with the author's permission)

We intended our book to achieve some of what Hongo's poem does—that we also "live for" stories that our children tell us, stories that they enact, stories of our children's families, and those professional stories that move us, that keep us connected to our teaching passions and goals. These stories consist of living words that, as Hongo writes, "can call up rain, could hymn like the sea"—they are words that conjure a sense of the mystery, magic, challenges, and joys of teaching and learning in classrooms and schools. Narrative inquiry, at its heart, is about words—the words we hear, the words we pay attention to, the words that guide us as individuals and as professionals dedicated to educational change and transformation.

AUTHORS' BIOGRAPHIES

Stephanie Sisk-Hilton is Associate Professor of Elementary Education at San Francisco State University. She teaches courses in science curriculum and instruction, child development, and teacher research. She received a BA in Cognitive Science from The Johns Hopkins University, a Masters Degree in Education Policy and Administration from Stanford University, and a PhD in Cognition and Development from The University of California, Berkeley. She has been an elementary and middle school teacher in Prince George's County, MD, Atlanta, GA, Brooklyn, NY, and Oakland, CA. She works extensively as a teacher professional developer dealing with school-wide curriculum reform and with science curriculum and pedagogy. Her research focuses on how children come to understand core ideas in science, and how issues of agency and belonging interact with content understanding. As part of her ongoing engagement in narrative inquiry for teaching, she teaches fourth- and fifth-grade environmental science and blogs at raisetheroofscience.com.

Daniel R. Meier is Professor of Elementary Education at San Francisco State University. Meier teaches in the MA Program in Early Childhood Education and the EdD Program in Educational Leadership. He teaches courses in reading/language arts, narrative inquiry and memoir, educational research, international education, first and second language development, and families and communities. He received his BA from Wesleyan University, EdM from Harvard University, and PhD from the University of California at Berkeley. He has written numerous articles and several books on teaching and learning, language and literacy, and reflective practice and teacher research. His current work focuses on early childhood teacher research groups in the San Francisco Bay Area and reflective practice in early childhood teacher education in the West Bank/Palestine.

REFERENCES

Ada, A. F. (2004). *With love, the little red hen*. New York, NY: Atheneum.

Adichie, C. (2009). The danger of a single story. New York, NY: TEDGlobal. Retrieved on November 5, 2015 from www.ted.com/talks/chimamanda_adichie_the_danger_of_a_single_story.html.

Akin, R., & Campano, G. (2009). Practitioners' voices in trying times: A readers' theatre script. In M. Cochran-Smith & S. L. Lytle (Eds.), *Inquiry as stance: Practitioner research for the next generation* (pp. 347–381). New York, NY: Teachers College Press.

Allen, M., & Coole, H. (2012). Experimenter confirmation bias and the correction of science misconceptions. *Journal of Science Teacher Education, 23*(4), 387–405.

Ballenger, C. (1999). *Teaching other people's children: Literacy in a bilingual classroom*. New York, NY: Teachers College Press.

Ballenger, C. (2009). *Puzzling moments, teachable moments*. New York, NY: Teachers College Press.

Barone, T. (2001). *Touching eternity: The enduring outcomes of teaching*. New York, NY: Teachers College Press.

Barrett, M. S., & Stauffer, S. L. (2012). Resonant work: Toward an ethic of narrative research. In M. S. Barret and S. L. Stauffer (Eds.), *Narrative soundings: An anthology of narrative inquiry in music education*. Dordrecht, the Netherlands: Springer.

Behlen, K. (2015). *Toddlers in nature* (Unpublished paper). San Francisco State University, San Francisco, CA.

Bell, L.A., & Roberts, R.A. (2010). The storytelling project model: A theoretical framework for critical examination of racism through the arts. *Teachers College Record, 112*(9), 2295-2319.

Berliner, D. C. (2002). (Comment) Educational research: The hardest science of all. *Educational Researcher, 31*(8), 18–20. Retrieved on November 24, 2015 from www.jstor.org/stable/3594389.

Boal, A. (1979). *Theatre of the oppressed*. New York, NY: Theatre Communications Group.

Bold, C. (2012). *Using narrative in research*. London, UK: SAGE.

Boylorn, R. (2011). Black kids' (B.K.) stories: Ta(l)king (about) race outside of the classroom. *Cultural Studies ↔ Critical Methodologies, 11*(1), 59–70.

Braid, D. (2006). "Doing good physics": Narrative and innovation in research. *Journal of Folklore Research, 43*(2), 149–173.

Brown, B. (2010). *Brené Brown: The power of vulnerability* [Video file]. Retrieved on November 1, 2015 from www.ted.com/talks/brene_brown_on_vulnerability?language=en.

Bruner, J. (1991). The narrative construction of reality. *Critical Inquiry, 18*(1), 1–21.

Bullough, R. V. (2014). Methods for studying beliefs: Teacher writing, scenarios, and metaphor analysis. In H. Fives & M. G. Gill (Eds.), *International handbook of research on teachers' beliefs* (pp. 150–170). New York, NY: Routledge.

Calkins, L. M. (2006). *Units of study for teaching writing: Grades 3–5*. Portsmouth, NH: Heinemann.

Castro, R. (2015). *What's your language?* (Unpublished paper). San Francisco State University, San Francisco, CA.

Chard, S. C. (1998). *The project approach: Developing the basic framework*. New York, NY: Scholastic, Inc.

Clandinin, D., & Connelly, F. (1998). Stories to live by: Narrative understandings of school reform. *Curriculum Inquiry, 28*(2), 149–164.

Clandinin, D., & Connelly, F. (1999). *Shaping a professional identity: Stories of educational practice*. London, ON: Althouse Press.

Clandinin, D. J., & Connelly, F. M. (2000). *Narrative inquiry: Experience and story in qualitative research*. San Francisco, CA: Jossey-Bass.

Clandinin, D. J., Pushor, D., & Murray Orr, A. (2007). Navigating sites for narrative inquiry. *Journal of Teacher Education, 58*, 21–35.

Clandinin, J. (2013). *Engaging in narrative inquiry*. Walnut Creek, CA: Left Coast Press.

Cochran-Smith, M., & Lytle, S. L. (Eds.). (1993). *Inside/outside: Teacher research and knowledge*. New York, NY: Teachers College Press.

Cochran-Smith, M., & Lytle, S. L. (1999). Relationships of knowledge and practice: Teacher learning in communities. *Review of Research in Education, 24*, 249–305.

Cochran-Smith, M., & Lytle, S. (2009). *Inquiry as stance: Practitioner research for the next generation*. New York, NY: Teachers College Press.

Coles, R. (1990). *The call of stories: Teaching and the moral imagination*. Boston, MA: Houghton-Mifflin.

Connelly, F. M., & Clandinin, D. H. (1990). Stories of experience and narrative inquiry. *Educational Researcher, 19*(5), 2–14.

Cooper, P. M. (2011). *The classrooms all young children need: Lessons in teaching from Vivian Paley*. Chicago, IL: University of Chicago Press.

Coulter, C., Michael, C., & Poynor, L. (2007). Storytelling as pedagogy: An unexpected outcome of narrative inquiry. *Curriculum Inquiry, 37*(2), 103–122.

Coulter, C. A., & Smith, M. L. (2009). The construction zone: Literary elements in narrative research. *Educational Researcher, 38*(8), 577–590.

Cowhey, M. (2008). Reading the class. In S. Nieto (Ed.), *Dear Paulo—Letters from those who dare teach* (pp. 10–16). Boulder, CO: Paradigm Publishers.

Crews, N. (2006). *Below*. New York, NY: Henry Holt & Co.

Delgado, R. (1989). Storytelling for oppositionists and others: A plea for narrative. *Michigan Law Review, 87*, 2411–2441.

Durrell, G. (1988). *A practical guide for the amateur naturalist*. New York, NY: Knopf.

Edwards, C., Gandini, L., & Forman, G. (Eds.). (2012). *The hundred languages of children the Reggio Emilia experience in transformation* (3rd ed.). Santa Barbara, CA: ABC-CLIO.

Edwards, C., & Rinaldi, C. (Eds.). (2009). *The diary of Laura: Perspectives on a Reggio Emilia diary*. St. Paul, MN: Red Leaf Press.

Egan, K. (1986). *Teaching as storytelling: An alternative approach to teaching and the curriculum in the elementary school*. Ontario, Canada: Althouse Press.

Egan, K. (1992). *Imagination in teaching and learning: The middle school years*. Chicago, IL: University of Chicago Press.

Egan, K. (2005). *An imaginative approach to teaching*. San Francisco, CA: Jossey-Bass.

Eisner, E., & Barone, T. (2011). *Arts-based research*. New York, NY and Thousand Oaks, CA: SAGE.

Elbaz-Luwisch, F. (2004). Immigrant teachers: Stories of self and place. *International Journal of Qualitative Studies in Education, 17*(3), 387–414.

Emerson, R. M., Fretz, R. I., & Shaw, L. L. (2011). *Writing ethnographic field notes* (2nd ed.). Chicago, IL: University of Chicago Press.

Engel, S. (1999). *Context is everything: The nature of memory*. New York, NY: Freeman.

Escamilla, M. (2013). *Collage-making: A medium to unleash children's creativity* (Unpublished manuscript). San Francisco State University, San Francisco, CA.

Ferreiro, E. (2003). *Essays on literacy: Past and present of the verbs to read and to write*. Toronto, Canada: Groundwood.

Fischer, M. M. J. (1986). Ethnicity and the post-modern arts of memory. In J. Clifford & G. E. Marcus (Eds.), *Writing culture: The poetics and politics of ethnography* (pp. 194–233). Berkeley, CA: University of California Press.

Freire, P. (1967/1976). *Education and the practice of freedom*. London, UK: Writers and Readers Publishing Cooperative.

Freire, P. (1996). Interview with Paulo Freire: An incredible conversation. Retrieved on December 5, 2015 from www.youtube.com/watch?v=aFWjnkFypFA&feature=related-.

Gadotti, M., & Torres, C. A. (2009). Paulo Freire: Education for development. *Development and Change, 40*(6), 1255–1267.

Gadzikowski, A. (2007). *Story dictation: A guide for early childhood professionals*. St. Paul, MN: Redleaf Press.

García, O., & Kleifgen, J. A. (2010). *Educating emergent bilinguals: Policies, programs, and practices for English language learners*. New York, NY: Teachers College Press.

Geertz, C. (1988). *Works and lives: The anthropologist as author*. Stanford, CA: Stanford University Press.

Gish, A. (2015). *Second step's social-emotional curriculum effects on first graders* (Unpublished master's thesis). San Francisco State University, San Francisco, CA.

Given, H., Kuh, L., LeeKeenan, D., Mardell, B., Redditt, S., & Twombly, S. (2010). Changing school culture: Using documentation to support collaborative inquiry. *Theory into Practice, 49*, 36–46.

Goeson, R. (2014). Finding our voices through narrative inquiry: Exploring a conflict of cultures. *Voices of Practitioners, 9*(1), 1–22.

Goswami, D., Lewis, C., Rutherford, M., & Waff, D. (2009). *Teacher inquiry: Approaches to language and literacy research*. New York, NY: Teachers College Press.

Goswami, D., & Rutherford, M. (2009). "What's going on here?": Seeking answers through teacher inquiry. In D. Goswami, C. Lewis, M. Rutherford, & D. Waff (Eds.), *Teacher inquiry: Approaches to language and literacy research* (pp. 1–11). New York, NY: Teachers College Press.

Goswami, D., & Stillman, P. R. (1987). *Reclaiming the classroom: Teacher research as an agency for change*. Upper Montclair, NJ: Boynton/Cook Publishers.

Gravett, E. (2015). *Bear and hare go fishing*. New York, NY: Simon & Schuster.

Hardy, B. (1977). Narrative as a primary act of mind. In M. Meek, A. Warlow, & G. Barton (Eds.), *The cool web: The pattern of children's reading* (pp. 12–23). London, UK: The Bodley Head.

Hart, P. S., & Nisbet, E. C. (2011). Boomerang effects in science communication: How motivated reasoning and identity cues amplify opinion polarization about climate mitigation policies. *Communication Research,* 0093650211416646.

Helm, J. H., & Katz, L. G. (2010). *Young investigators: The project approach in the early years* (2nd ed.). New York, NY: Teachers College Press.

Hong, M., & Genishi, C. (2005). Voices of English language learners. In L. D. Soto & B. B. Swadener (Eds.), *Power and voice in research with children* (pp. 164–175). New York, NY: Peter Lang.

Hongo, G. (1995). *Volcano—A memoir of Hawai'i.* New York, NY: Knopf.

hooks, b. (2008). *Belonging: A culture of place.* New York, NY: Routledge.

Hubbard, R. S., & Power, B. M. (2003). *The art of classroom inquiry: A handbook for teacher-researchers (Revised ed.).* Portsmouth, NH: Heinemann.

Huber, J., Caine, V., Huber, M., & Steeves, P. (2013). Narrative inquiry as pedagogy in education: The extraordinary potential of living, telling, retelling, and reliving stories of experience. *Review of Research in Education, 37*(1), 212–242.

Jalongo, M. R., & Isenberg, J. P. (1993). Teachers' stories: Reflections on teaching, caring, and learning. *Childhood Education, 69*(5), 260–261.

Jalongo, M. R. (1995). *Teachers' stories: From personal narrative to professional insight.* San Francisco, CA: Jossey-Bass.

Jayewardene, G. (2013). Overcoming our fears—Embarking on a nature journey. In D. Meier & S. Sisk-Hilton (Eds.), *Nature education with young children: Integrating inquiry and practice* (pp. 99–112). New York, NY: Routledge.

Jimenez, S. (2015). *Emergent writers: TK can write!* (Unpublished paper). San Francisco State University, San Francisco, CA.

Johnson, K. E., & Golombek, P. R. (2002). Inquiry into experience: Teachers' personal and professional growth. In K. E. Johnson & P. R. Golombek (Eds.), *Teachers' narrative inquiry as professional development* (pp. 1–14). New York, NY: Cambridge University Press.

Jones, E., & Nimmo, J. (1994). *Emergent curriculum.* Washington, DC: NAEYC.

Jones, E. (2012). The emergence of emergent curriculum. *Young Children, 67*(2), 66–68.

Jones, S. H. (1998). Autoethnography: Making the personal political. In N. K. Denzin & Y. S. Lincoln (Eds.), *Collecting and interpreting qualitative materials* (3rd ed.) (pp. 205–246). Thousand Oaks, CA: SAGE.

Kastle, C. (2012). *Early childhood teacher research: From questions to results.* New York, NY: Routledge.

Katz, L. G., Chard, S. C., & Kogan, Y. (2014). *Engaging children's minds: The project approach* (3rd edition). Santa Barbara, CA: Praeger.

Kohl, H. (1998). *The discipline of hope: Learning from a lifetime of teaching.* New York, NY: The New Press.

Kroll, L. (2012). *Self-study and inquiry into practice: Learning to teach for equity and social justice in the elementary school classroom.* New York, NY: Routledge.

Kroll, L. R., & Meier, D. R. (Eds.). (2015). *Educational change in international early childhood contexts: Crossing borders of reflection.* New York, NY: Routledge.

Ladson-Billings, G. (2007). Pushing past the achievement gap: An essay on the language of deficit. *Journal of Negro Education, 76*(3), 316–325.

Lampert, M. (2003). *Teaching problems and the problems of teaching.* New Haven, CT: Yale University Press.

Lawrence-Lightfoot, S., & Davis, J. H. (1997). *The art and science of portraiture.* San Francisco, CA: Jossey-Bass.

Lawrence-Lightfoot, S. (2005). Reflections on portraiture: A dialogue between art and science. *Qualitative Inquiry, 11*(1), 3–15.

Lawrence-Lightfoot, S., & Hoffmann Davis, J. (1997). *The art and science of portraiture*. San Francisco, CA: Jossey-Bass.

Lewis, C. (2009). Using narrative as teacher research: Learning about language and life through personal stories. In D. Goswami, C. Lewis, M. Rutherford, & D. Waff (Eds.), *Teacher inquiry: Approaches to language and literacy research* (pp. 43–68). New York, NY: Teachers College Press.

Lewis, C., & Tsuchida, I. (1998). A lesson is like a swiftly flowing river: How research lessons improve Japanese education. *American Educator, 22*(4), 50–53.

Lightfoot, S. L. (1983). *The good high school: Portraits of character and culture*. New York, NY: Basic Books.

Lin, G. (1999). *Ugly vegetables*. Watertown, MA: Charlesbridge.

Loseke, D. R. (2007). The study of identity as cultural, institutional, organizational, and personal narrative: Theoretical and empirical integrations. *Sociological Quarterly, 48*(4), 661–688.

Loughran, J., & Russell, T. (Eds.). (2002). *Improving teacher education practices through self-study*. New York, NY: Routledge.

Lyons, N., & LaBoskey, V. (Eds.). (2002). *Narrative inquiry in practice*. New York, NY: Teachers College Press.

Macdonald, H. (2015). *H is for hawk*. New York, NY: Vintage.

McNamee, G. D. (2005). "The one who gathers children:" The work of Vivian Gussin Paley and current debates about how we educate young children. *Journal of Early Childhood Teacher Education, 25*(3), 275–296.

McNeill, L. (2003). Teaching an old genre new tricks: The diary on the internet. *Biography, 26*(1), 24–47.

Meier, D. R. (1997). *Learning in small moments: Life in an urban classroom*. New York, NY: Teachers College Press.

Meier, D. R. (2000). *Scribble scrabble: Learning to read and write—Success with diverse teachers, children, and families*. New York, NY: Teachers College Press.

Meier, D. R., & Henderson, B. (2007). *Learning from young children in the classroom: The art and science of teacher research*. New York, NY: Teachers College Press.

Merriam, S. B. (1998). *Qualitative research and case study applications in education: Revised and expanded from case study research in research* (2nd ed.). San Francisco, CA: Jossey-Bass.

Myers, C. (2013). Young dreamers. *The Horn Book, 89*(6), 10–14.

Nardi, B. A., Schiano, D. J., & Gumbrecht, M. (2004). Blogging as social activity, or, would you let 900 million people read your diary? Chicago, IL: Computers Supported Cooperative Network.

National Association for the Education of Young Children (NAEYC) (2012). *The common core standards: Caution and opportunity for early childhood education*. Washington, D.C.: National Association for the Education of Young Children.

NGSS Lead States. (2013). *Next Generation Science Standards: For states, by states*. Washington, DC: The National Academies Press.

Nyhan, B., Reifler, J., & Ubel, P. A. (2013). The hazards of correcting myths about health care reform. *Medical Care, 51*(2), 127–132.

Pagnucci, G. (2004). *Living the narrative life: Stories as a tool for meaning making*. Portsmouth, NH: Heinemann.

Paley, V. (1981). *Wally's stories*. Cambridge, MA: Harvard University Press.

Paley, V. G. (1990). *The boy who would be a helicopter*. Cambridge, MA: Harvard University Press.

Perry, G., Henderson, B., & Meier, D. R. (Eds.). (2012). *Our inquiry, our practice: Undertaking, supporting, and learning from early childhood teacher research(ers)*. Washington, DC: National Association for the Education of Young Children.

Peters-Hoyte, K. J. (2015, December 11). Shifting my thinking/shifting their achievement: An asset approach to African American male readers [Web log post]. Retrieved from http://millsscholars.org/shifting-my-thinking-shifting-their-achievement-an-asset-approach-to-supporting-african-american-male-readers/.

Phillips, A., & Gallas, K. (2004). Introduction: Developing a community of inquiry: The values and practices of the Brookline teacher researcher seminar. In C. Ballenger (Ed.), *Regarding children's words: Teacher research on language and literacy, Brookline teacher researcher seminar* (pp. 3–6). New York, NY: Teachers College Press.

Pohio, L., Sansom, A., & Liley, K. A. (2015). My past is my present is my future: A bicultural approach to early years education in Aotearoa, New Zealand. In L. R. Kroll & D. R. Meier (Eds.), *Educational change in international early childhood contexts: Crossing borders of reflection* (pp. 103–122). New York, NY: Routledge.

Polkinghorne, D. E. (1988). *Narrative knowing and the human sciences*. Albany, NY: SUNY Press.

Pushor, D., & Clandinin, D. J. (2009). The interconnections between narrative inquiry and action research. In S. Noffke & B. Somekh (Eds.), *The SAGE handbook of educational action research* (pp. 290–300). Thousand Oaks, CA: SAGE.

Quintero, E. (2015). Connecting funds of knowledge to the curriculum. In E. P. Quintero & M. K. Rummel (Eds.), *Storying a path to our future: Artful thinking, learning, teaching, & research* (pp. 47–57). New York, NY: Peter Lang.

Reddick, R. J., & Saénz, V. B. (2012). Coming home: *Hermanos académicos* reflect on past and present realities as professors at their alma mater. *Harvard Educational Review, 82*(3), 353–380.

Rendon, L. I. (2009). *Sensipensante (sensing/thinking pedagogy): Educating for wholeness, justice, and liberation*. Sterling, VA: Stylus Publishing.

Ricouer, P. (1988). *Time and narrative (vol. 3)*. Chicago, IL: University of Chicago Press.

Riessman, C. K. (2008). *Narrative methods for the human sciences*. Los Angeles: SAGE.

Rifkin, J. (2009). *The empathic civilization: The race to global consciousness in a world in crisis*. New York, NY: Penguin.

Rinaldi, C. (2001). Documentation and assessment: What is the relationship? In C. Giudici, M. Krechevsky, & C. Rinaldi (Eds.), *Making learning visible: Children as individuals and group learners* (pp. 78–90). Reggio Emilia, Italy: Reggio Children.

Rios, V. (2011). *Punished: Policing the lives of Black and Latino boys*. New York, NY: New York University Press.

Rowbottom, D., & Aiston, S. (2006). The myth of "scientific method" in contemporary educational research. *Journal of Philosophy of Education, 40*(2), 137–156.

Sahlberg, P. (2014). *Finnish lessons 2.0: What can the world learn from educational change in Finland?* New York, NY: Teachers College Press.

Seidman, I. (2013). *Interviewing as qualitative research* (4th ed.). New York, NY: Teachers College Press.

Soto, L. D. (2008). *Making a difference in the lives of bilingual/bicultural children*. New York, NY: Peter Lang.

Souto-Manning, M. (2006). Voices: Community, parents, teachers, and students. *Journal of Latinos and Education, 5*(4), 293–304.

Souto-Manning, M. (2007). Immigrant families and children (re)develop identities in a new context. *Early Childhood Education Journal, 34*(6), 399–405.

Souto-Manning, M., & Ray, N. (2007). Beyond survival in the ivory tower: Black and brown women's living narratives. *Equity & Excellence in Education, 40*(4), 280–290.

Speedy, J. (2008). *Narrative inquiry and psychotherapy*. New York, NY: Palgrave.

Stremmel, A. (2014). The power of narrative inquiry to transform both teacher and mentor. *Voices of Practioners, 9*(1), 1–5.

Strong-Wilson, T. (2006). Re-visioning one's narratives: Exploring the relationship between researcher self-study and teacher research. *Studying Teacher Education, 2*(1), 59–76.

Tan, A. (1990). Mother tongue. *Threepenny Review, 11*(3), 1–4.

Valente, J. M. (2011). *d/Deaf and d/Dumb: A portrait of a deaf kid as a young superhero*. Peter Lang: New York.

Wien, C. (2008). *Emergent curriculum in the primary classroom: Interpreting the Reggio Emilia approach in schools*. New York, NY: Teachers College Press.

Willingham, D. T. (2004). The privileged status of story. *American Educator, 28*, 43–45.

Windschitl, M., Thompson, J., & Braaten, M. (2008). Beyond the scientific method: Model-based inquiry as a new paradigm of preference for school science investigations. *Science Education, 92*(5), 941–967.

Winn, M. (2010). "Betwixt and between": Literacy, liminality, and the celling of Black girls. *Race Ethnicity and Education, 13*(4), 425–447.

Winn, M. (2011). *Girl time: Literacy, justice, and the school-to-prison pipeline*. New York, NY: Teachers College Press.

Witherell, C. (2004). Introduction. In R. J. Nash (Ed.), *Liberating scholarly narrative: The power of personal narrative* (pp. vii–viii). New York, NY: Teachers College Press.

Wright, T. (2010). Learning to laugh: A portrait of risk and resilience in early childhood. *Harvard Educational Review, 80*(4), 444–463.

Young, A. Y, Barrett, R., Young-Rivera, Y., & Lovejoy, K. M. (2014). *Other people's English: Code-meshing, code-switching, and African-American literacy*. New York, NY: Teachers College Press.

Zeichner, K. M. (1994). Research on teacher thinking and different views of reflective practice in teaching and teacher education. In I. Carlgren, G. Handal, & S. Vaage (Eds.), *Teachers' minds and actions: Research on teachers' thinking and practice* (pp. 9–27). London, UK: The Falmer Press.

Zeichner, K. M., & Liston, D. P. (1998). *Reflective teaching: An introduction*. Mahwah, NJ: Lawrence Erlbaum.

Zeichner, K. M., & Liston, D. P. (2014). *Reflective teaching: An introduction* (2nd ed.). New York, NY: Routledge.

Zwinger, S. (1998). Overlooking Carrizo Gorge. In S. Gilbar (Ed.), *Natural state: A literary anthology of California nature writing* (pp. 213–218). Berkeley, CA: University of California Press.

INDEX